The Psychology Of Salesmanship

William Walker Atkinson

SANAGE
PUBLISHING HOUSE

Paperback: 978-939-0896-61-5

Printed by:
Sanage Publishing House LLP
Mumbai, India
sanagepublishing@gmail.com

Designed by:
allpublishingsolution.com

CONTENTS

CHAPTER 1

PSYCHOLOGY IN BUSINESS

Until the last few years the mere mention of the word "psychology" in connection with business was apt to be greeted with a shrug of the shoulders, a significant raising of the eyebrows—and a change of the subject. Psychology was a subject that savored of the class room, or else was thought to be somehow concerned with the soul, or possibly related to the abnormal phenomena generally classified as "psychic." The average business man was apt to impatiently resent the introduction into business of class room topics, or speculation regarding the soul, or of theories and tales regarding clairvoyance, telepathy, or general "spookiness"—for these were the things included in his concept of "psychology."

But a change has come to the man in business. He has heard much of late years regarding psychology in business affairs, and has read something on the subject. He understands now that psychology means "the science of the mind" and is not necessarily the same as metaphysics or "psychism." He has had brought home to him the fact that psychology plays a most important part in business, and that it is quite worth his while to acquaint himself with its fundamental principles. In fact, if he has thought sufficiently on the subject, he will have seen that the entire process of selling goods, personally, or by means of advertising or display, is essentially a mental process depending upon the state of mind induced in the purchaser, and that these states of mind are induced solely by reason of certain established principles of psychology. Whether the salesman, or advertiser, realizes this or not, he is employing psychological principles in attracting the attention, arousing the interest, creating the desire, and moving the will of the purchaser of his goods.

The best authorities on salesmanship and advertising now recognize this fact and emphasize it in their writings. George

French, in his "*Art and Science of Advertising*" says regarding psychology in advertising: "So we can dismiss the weird word, and simply acknowledge that we can sell things to a man more readily if we know the man. We can't personally know every man to whom we wish to sell goods. We must therefore consider if there are not certain ways of thinking and of acting which are common to all men, or to a large proportion of men. If we can discover the laws governing the action of men's minds we will know how to appeal to those men. We know how to appeal to Smith, because we know Smith. We know what will please Brown, because we know Brown. We know how to get our way with Jones, because we know Jones. What the advertiser must know is how to get at Smith, Brown, and Jones without knowing any of them. While every man has his personal peculiarities, and while every mind has its peculiar method of dealing with the facts of life, every man and every mind is controlled, in a large sense and to a great extent, by predilections and mind-workings which were established before he lived, and are operated in a manner separate from his personality. Our minds are more automatic, more mechanical, than we are willing to admit. That which we loosely call mind is largely the automatic expression of tendencies controlled by physical conditions wholly apart from conscious intellectual or moral motives or qualities. What those physical conditions are, and how the knowledge of what they are may be utilized by advertisers, forms the body of that new knowledge some like to call psychology, so far as it concerns advertising." Mr. French has well expressed the idea of the important part played in business by psychology. What he says is, of course, as applicable to personal salesmanship as to salesmanship through advertisements—the same principles are present and operative in both cases.

In order to bring to the mind of the reader the full idea of the operation of psychological principles in the sale of goods, we shall mention a few particular instances in which these principles have played a part. Each reader will be able to recollect many similar instances, once his attention is called to the matter.

Prof. Halleck, a well known authority on psychology says: "Business men say that the ability to gain the attention is often the secret of success in life. Enormous salaries are paid to persons who can write advertisements certain to catch the eye. A publisher said that he had sold only five thousand copies of an excellent work, merely because it had failed to catch the attention of many, and that twenty-five thousand copies could have been disposed of in the same time, if agents had forced them upon the notice of people. Druggists say that any kind of patent medicine can be sold, if it is so advertised as to strike the attention in a forcible manner. Business life has largely resolved itself into a battle to secure the attention of people."

The same excellent authority says, regarding the effect of associated ideas: "An eminent philosopher has said that man is completely at the mercy of the association of his ideas. Every new object is seen in the light of its associated ideas. * * * The principle of the association of ideas is sufficient to account for the change in fashions. A woman in a southern city had a bonnet that she particularly admired, until she one day saw three negresses wearing precisely the same pattern. She never appeared again in that bonnet. When a style of dress becomes 'common,' and is worn by the lower classes, it is discarded by the fashionable people. Fashions that are absolutely repulsive will often be adopted if they are introduced by popular or noted people. * * * A knowledge of the power of the association of ideas is of the utmost importance in business. One man has his store so planned that all its associations are pleasing, from the manner of the clerks to the fixtures and drapery. Another store brings up unpleasant associations. * * * When negligee hats first made their appearance, a shrewd hatter sent for a well-dressed and popular collegian and offered him his choice of the best hats in the store, if he would wear a negligee hat for three days. He objected to making such an exhibition of himself, until he was flattered by the hatter's wager that the hats could, in this way, be made the fashion for the entire town. When the collegian first put in his appearance on the campus with the hat, he was guyed for his oddity. Late in the afternoon, some of his friends concluded that the hat looked so well that they would invest. On the following day large numbers reached the same conclusion. For some time after this the hatter found difficulty in keeping a sufficient supply in stock. Had an unpopular or poorly dressed man appeared first on the campus with that hat, the result would have been the reverse. The hat would have been the same, but the association of ideas would have differed. Some of the ladies of fashion in a large European city selected on their own responsibility, without consulting the milliners, a cheap spring Manilla hat, which was very handsome. The milliners found themselves with a high-priced stock for which there was no demand. They held a council, bought a large number of the cheap hats, and put them on the heads of all the female street sweepers and scavengers in the town. When the ladies of fashion went out the next day, they were amazed to see the very dregs of the city arrayed in headgear like their own. It was not very long before the result was what might have been expected."

In a previous work of the present writer, the following illustrations of the effect of psychological suggestion in advertising were used:

The use of the "direct command" as the "ad. men" call it, is very common. People are positively told to do certain things in these advertisements. They are told to "take home a cake of Hinky-dink's Soap tonight; your wife needs it!" And they do it. Or they see a mammoth hand pointing down at them from a sign, and almost hear the corresponding mammoth voice as it says (in painted words): "Say you! Smoke Honey-Dope Cigars; they're the best ever!!!" And, if you manage to reject the command the first time, you will probably yield at the repeated suggestion of the same thing being hurled at you at every corner and high fence, and "Honey-Dope" will be your favorite brand until some other suggestion catches you. Suggestion by authority and repetition, remember; that's what does the business for you! They call this the "Direct Command" in the advertising schools. Then there are some other subtle forms of suggestion in advertising. You see staring from every bit of space, on billboard and in newspapers and magazines: "Uwanta Cracker," or something of that sort—and you usually wind up by acquiescing. And then you are constantly told that "Babies howl for Grandma Hankin's Infantile Soother," and then when you hear some baby howling you think of what you have been told they are howling for, and then you run and buy a bottle of "Grandma Hankin's." Then you are told that some cigar is "Generously Liberal" in size and quality; or that some kind of Cocoa is "Grateful and Refreshing"; or that some brand of soap is "99.999% Pure"; etc., etc. Only last night I saw a new one—"Somebody's Whisky is Smooth," and every imbiber in the car was smacking his lips and thinking about the "smooth" feeling in his mouth and throat. It *was* smooth—the idea, not the stuff, I mean. And some other whiskey man shows a picture of a glass, a bottle, some ice and a syphon of seltzer, with simply these words: "Oldboy's Highball—That's all!" All of these things are suggestions, and some of them are very powerful ones, too, when constantly impressed upon the mind by repetition. * * * I have known dealers in Spring goods to force the season by filling their windows with their advance stock. I have seen hat dealers start up the straw hat season by putting on a straw themselves, their clerks ditto, and then a few friends. The sprinkling of "straws" gave a suggestion to the street, and the straw hat season was opened.

Dr. Herbert A. Parkyn, an authority on Suggestion, draws the following picture from life of a retail merchant who is suffering from the effect of adverse psychological influences resulting from his pessimistic mental attitude. The present writer can vouch for the accuracy of Dr. Parkyn's picture, for he knows the original of the sketch. Dr. Parkyn says of the storekeeper:

"He is the proprietor of a store in a neighboring city; but such a store—it almost gives me the blues to go into it! His windows are dressed year in and year out with the same old signs, and there is nothing to give the store the cheerful appearance so essential to an up-to-date business establishment. But the atmosphere of the place is only in keeping with the proprietor. When he started in business thirty years ago he employed eight clerks, but his business has fallen off till he does all the work himself and is scarcely able now to pay rent, although competitors around him are increasing their business steadily every year. In the course of a fifteen minute's conversation, the first time I met him, he told me all his troubles, which were many. According to his story, everyone had been trying to get the better of him ever since he started in business; his competitors resorted to unfair business methods; his landlord was endeavoring to drive him out by raising his rent; he could not get an honest clerk in his store; an old man had not an equal chance with a young man; he could not understand why people he had catered to so faithfully should be so ungrateful or so fickle as to give their patronage to every upstart who went into business in the same line as his; he supposed that he could work along, as he was doing, from morning till night without a holiday till he was driven to the poorhouse or died, and although he had been in the same stand for fifteen years there was not a single person he could call on if in need of a friend, etc. Although I have had occasion to visit him many times during business hours, I have never heard him address a cheerful or encouraging remark to a customer. On the other hand he waited on them, not only with an air of indifference, but apparently as if he were doing them a favor by allowing them to trade at his store, while others who dropped in to ask permission to use his telephone or to enquire about residents in the neighborhood were soon given to understand by his manner and answers that he considered them a nuisance and hoped they had not mistaken his store for an information bureau. I have purposely led him into other channels of conversation, with the same result; everything was going to the dogs—the city, the country, etc. No matter what was talked about, his remarks were saturated with pessimism. He was ready to blame everything and everyone for his condition, and when I ventured to suggest that much of his trouble was due to his attitude he was ready to show me to the door. * * * If he would but cast his bread upon the waters for a few weeks by bestowing a smile here and a smile there, or a cheerful encouraging word to this customer and that customer, he would certainly feel better for the giving, and they would return to him a thousand fold. If he would only assume that he is prosperous and proceed to give his store an air of prosperity, how much more attractive he could make his place look and how much more inviting it would be for customers! If he would assume that every person that entered his store was his guest, whether he made a purchase or not, people would feel like returning to his store when they wanted anything in his line. I could suggest a hundred ways in which this man could employ suggestion and auto-suggestion to increase his business, to draw friends to him, instead of driving them away, and to make the world and himself better and happier while he lives in it."

But, you may ask, what has all this to do with psychology in salesmanship—what has the matter of advertising, store display, personal manner, etc., to do with salesmanship? Just this much, that all these things are based on the same fundamental principles as is salesmanship, and that these fundamental principles are those of psychology. All that has been said refers to psychology—all is the effect of psychology pure and simple. All depends upon the mental attitude, the suggestions offered, the mental states induced, the motive to the will—all these outward things are merely the effects of inner mental states.

J.W. Kennedy, in "Judicious Advertising" says: "Advertising is just salesmanship on paper; a mere money-making means of selling goods rapidly. That 'mysterious something' is just printed persuasion and its other name is 'selling conviction.' Conviction can be imparted at will by those few writers who have closely studied the thought processes by which conviction is induced. The mission of every ad. is to convert readers into buyers." Geo. Dyers, in the same journal says: "Advertising takes into account the sub- conscious impressions, the varying phases of suggestion and association as received through the eye, the psychology of the direct command,—all worth earnest consideration, and seriously to be reckoned with, however we may balk at the terms." Seth Brown in "Salesmanship" says: "To make advertising which will sell goods requires development of the human part of the writer. He must realize the different forces which command Attention, Interest, Desire and Conviction. The buyer wants your goods because they will produce for him some definite effect or result. It is this result that the ad. man must keep in mind."

"But," you may also say, "after all this 'psychology' seems to be nothing else than what we have always known as 'human nature'—there is nothing new about this." Exactly so! Psychology is the inner science of human nature. Human nature depends entirely upon psychological processes—it is bound up with the activities of the mind. The study of human nature is the study of the minds of people. But whereas the study of human nature, as usually conducted, is a haphazard, hit-or-miss sort of undertaking, the study of the mind, according to the established principles of psychology, is of the nature of the study of science, and is pursued according to scientific methods.

Particularly in its phase of Salesmanship does the study of human nature along the lines of psychology become a science. From the first to the last Salesmanship is a psychological subject. Every step in the process of a sale is a mental process. The mental attitude and mental expression of the salesman; the mental attitude and mental impression of the customer; the process of arousing the attention, awakening curiosity or interest, creating desire, satisfying the reason, and moving the will—all these are purely mental processes, and the study of them becomes a branch of the study of psychology. The display of goods on the counters, shelves, or windows of a store, or in the hands of the salesman on the road, must be based upon psychological principles. The argument of the salesman must not only be logical but must be so arranged and worded as to arouse certain feelings or faculties within the mind of the prospective buyer—this is psychology. And finally, the closing of the sale, in which the object is to arouse the will of the buyer into final favorable action—this also is psychology. From the entrance of the salesman to the final closing of the sale, each and every step is a psychological process. A sale is the action and reaction of mind upon mind, according to well established psychological principles and rules. Salesmanship is essentially a psychological science as all must admit who will give to the subject a logical consideration. To those who object to the term "psychology" because of its newness and unfamiliar sound, we do not care to urge the term. Let such cling to their old term of "human nature," remembering however that "human nature" is essentially mental. A dead man, a man asleep or in a trance, or an idiot, manifests no "human nature" in the sense the word is generally used. A man must be alive, wide awake, and in possession of his senses, before he is able to manifest "human nature," and before his "human nature" may be appealed to according to the well known principles. "Human nature" cannot be divorced from psychology, try as we may.

We do not for a moment wish to imply that Salesmanship is entirely dependent upon a knowledge of psychology. There are other factors concerned. For instance, the salesman must possess a practical knowledge of his goods; of the seasons; of the trend of fashion in relation to his line; of the adaptability of certain goods for certain sections. But, waiving for the moment the point that even these are concerned with the mind of people at the last, and admitting that they may be considered as independent of psychology, all of these points will avail nothing if the salesman violates the psychological principles of the sale. Give such a man the best goods, of the best house, with a thorough knowledge of the requirements of the trade and the goods themselves, and send him forth to sell those goods. The result will be that his sales will fall below the mark of a man far less well equipped in other respects but who understands the psychology of salesmanship, either intuitively or else by conscious acquirement.

Inasmuch as the essence of Salesmanship is the employment of the proper psychological principles, does it not seem imperative that the salesman should know something of the Mind of Man—the instrument upon which he must play in plying his vocation? Should not the salesman possess the same kind of knowledge of his instrument as does the musician, the mechanic, the artisan, the artist? What would be thought of one who would expect to become an expert swordsman without a knowledge of the principles of fencing, or of one who would expect to become a boxer without mastering the established principle of boxing? The instruments of the salesman are his own mind and the mind of his customers. He should acquaint himself thoroughly with both.

CHAPTER 2

THE MIND OF THE SALESMAN

In the Psychology of Salesmanship there are two important elements, viz: (1) The Mind of the Salesman; and (2) the Mind of the Buyer. The proposition, or the goods to be sold, constitute the connecting link between the two Minds, or the common point upon which the two Minds must unite, blend, and come to agreement. The Sale itself is the result of the fusion and agreement of the two Minds—the product of the action and reaction between them. Let us now proceed to a consideration of the two important elements, the Two Minds involved in the process of Salesmanship.

Beginning our consideration of the Mind of the Salesman, let us realize that upon his mind depends his character and personality. His character is composed of his individual mental qualities or attributes. His personality is his customary outward expression of his character. Both character and personality may be altered, changed and improved. And there is in each person a central *something* which he calls "I," which is able to order and manifest these changes in his character and personality. While it may be argued plausibly that a man is merely a composite of his characteristics and nothing more, nevertheless there is always in each the consciousness that in his real "I" there is a something which is above and behind characteristics, and which may regulate the latter. Without attempting to lead the reader into the maze of metaphysics, or the pitfalls of philosophy, we wish to impress upon him the fact that his mental being has for its innermost centre of consciousness this mysterious "I," the nature of which no one has ever been able to determine, but which when fully realized imparts to one a strength and force undreamed of before.

And it is well worth while for everyone seeking self-development and self- improvement to awaken to a clear realization of this "I" within him, to which every faculty, every quality, every characteristic is an instrument of expression and manifestation. The real "you" is not the characteristics or features of personality, which change from time to time, but a permanent, changeless, centre and background of the changes of personality—a something that endures through all changes, and which you simply know as "I." In the volume of this series, entitled "*The New Psychology*," in the chapter entitled "The Ego, or Self" we have spoken of this in detail. Further mention would be out of place in the present volume, but we may be pardoned for quoting the following from the said chapter, for we feel that a realization of this "I" is most important to each person who wishes to master his own mind, and to create his own personality. Here follows the quotation:

"The consciousness of the 'I' is above personality—it is something inseparable from individuality. * * * The consciousness of the 'I' is an actual experience, just as much as is the consciousness of the page before you. * * * The whole subject of The New Psychology is bound up with this recognition of the 'I'—it revolves around this 'I' as a wheel around its centre. We regard the mental faculties, powers, organs, qualities, and modes of expression, as merely instruments, tools, or channels of expression of this wonderful Something—the Self, the pure Ego—the 'I.' And this is the message of The New Psychology—that You, the 'I,' have at your command a wonderful array of mental instruments, tools, machinery, which if properly used will create for you any kind of personality you may desire. You are the Master Workman who may make of yourself what you will. But before you can appreciate this truth—before you can make it your own—before you can apply it—you must enter into a recognition and realization of this wonderful 'I' that you are, to which body and senses, yea, even the mind itself, are but channels of expression. You are something more than body, or senses, or mind—you are that wonderful Something, master of all these things, but of which you can say but one thing: 'I AM.'"

But remember, always, that this realization of the Ego does not mean egotism, or self-conceit, or comparison of your character or personality with that of others. It is Egoism not Egotism—and Egoism means simply the realization of this "Master-Consciousness" to which all other mental faculties are subordinate. If you want some other name for it, you may consider this "I" as the "Will of the will," for it is the very essence of *will-power*—it is, so to speak, the Will conscious of itself. By means of the realization, you will find it far easier to cultivate the mental qualities in which you are deficient, and to restrain undesirable characteristics. The spirit of the idea may be gained by a careful understanding of the following from the pen of Charles F. Lummis: "I'm all right. I am bigger than anything that can happen to me. All these things are outside my door, *and I've got the key*!"

The mental qualities most requisite to the Salesman may be stated as follows:

I. *Self Respect.* It is important to the Salesman that he cultivate the faculty of Self Respect. By this we do not mean egotism, conceit, superciliousness, imperiousness, hauteur, snobbishness, etc., all of which are detrimental qualities. Self Respect, on the contrary imparts the sense of true manhood or womanhood, self-reliance, dignity, courage and independence. It is the spirit of Black Hawk, the Indian chieftain, who, lifting his head said to Jackson: "I am a Man!" It is entirely opposed to the crawling, cringing "worm of the dust," mental attitude of Uriah Heep, who was continually asserting how humble—how very humble—he was. Learn to look the world in the eyes without flinching. Throw off the fear of the crowd, and the impression that you are unworthy. Learn to believe in yourself, and to respect yourself. Let your motto be "I Can; I Will; I Dare; I Do!"

Self Respect is a sure antidote for the feeling of fear, shrinking, sense of inferiority, and other negative feelings which sometimes oppress the Salesman when he is about to enter into the presence of some "big man." Remember that the man's personality is merely a mask, and that behind it is merely an "I" like your own—no more, no less. Remember that behind the "John Smith" part of you there exists the same kind of "I" that exists behind the "High Mucky-muck" part of him. Remember that you are Man approaching Man—not a worm approaching a god. Remember that just as Kipling says: "The Colonel's lady and Judy O'Grady *are sisters under their skin*," so are you and the big man twin "I's" beneath the covering of personality, position, and outward appearance. By cultivating the realization of the "I," of which we have told you, you will acquire a new sense of Self Respect which will render you immune from the feeling of bashfulness, inferiority and fear in the presence of others. Unless a man respects himself, he cannot expect others to respect him. He should build up his true individuality and respect it, being careful, always, not to get "side-tracked" by egotism, vanity and similar follies of personality. It is not your personality which is entitled to respect, but your *individuality*, which is something far different. The personality belongs to the outer man, the individuality to the inner.

One's physical carriage and attitude tends to react upon his own mental attitude as well as also impressing those in whose presence he is. There is always an action and reaction between mind and body. Just as mental states take form in physical actions, so do physical actions react upon the mind and influence mental states. Frown continually and you will feel cross; smile and you will feel cheerful. Carry yourself like a man, and you will feel like a man. Carl H. Pierce says regarding the proper carriage of a salesman: "Remember that you are asking no favors; that you have nothing to apologize for, and that you have every reason in the world to hold your head up high. And it is wonderful what this holding of the head will do in the way of increasing sales.

We have seen salesmen get entrance to the offices of Broadway buyers simply through the holding of the head straight up from the shoulders. The rule to follow is: Have your ear lobes directly over your shoulders, so that a plumb line hung from the ears describes the line of your body. Be sure not to carry the head either to the right or left but vertical. Many men make the mistake, especially when waiting for a prospect to finish some important piece of business, of leaning the head either to the right or left. This indicates weakness. A study of men discloses the fact that the strong men never tilt the head. Their heads sit perfectly straight on strong necks. Their shoulders, held easily yet firmly in correct position, are inspiring in their strength indicating poise. Every line of the body, in other words, denotes the thought of the bearer."

So cultivate not only the inner sense of Self Respect, but also the outward indications of that mental state. Thus do you secure the benefit of the action and reaction between body and mind.

II. *Poise.* The salesman should cultivate Poise, which manifests in balance, tranquility and ease. Poise is that mental quality which maintains a natural balance between the various faculties, feelings, emotions and tendencies. It is the assertion of the "I" as the Master and controller of the mental states, feelings, and action. Poise enables one to correctly *balance* himself, mentally, instead of allowing his feelings or emotions to run away with him. Poise enables one to remain the Master of Himself, instead of "slopping over" on the one hand, or of "losing his nerve" on the other. Poise enables one to "keep himself well in hand." The man who has Poise indeed has Power, for he is never thrown off his balance, and consequently always remains master of the situation. Did you ever hear of, or see, the Gyroscope? Well, it is a peculiar little mechanical contrivance consisting of a whirling wheel within a frame work, the peculiarity consisting of the arrangement and action of the wheel which by its motion always maintains its balance and equilibrium. No matter how the little apparatus is turned, it always maintains its equilibrium. It is likely to play an important part in aerial navigation and mono-rail systems of transportation, in the future.

Well, here is the point—*be a Mental Gyroscope.* Cultivate the mental quality which acts automatically in the direction of keeping your balance and centre of mental gravity. This does not mean that you should be a prig, or a solemn-faced smug bore, with an assumption of supernatural dignity. On the contrary, always be natural in manner and action. The point is to always maintain your balance, and mental control, instead of allowing your feelings or emotions to run away with you. Poise means Mastery—lack of it means Slavery. As Edward Carpenter says: "How rare indeed to meet a *man*! How common rather to discover a creature hounded on by tyrant thoughts (or cares, or desires), cowering, wincing under the lash—or perchance priding himself to run merrily in obedience to a driver that rattles the reins and persuades himself that he is free." Poise is the Mental Gyroscope—keep it in good working order.

III. *Cheerfulness.* The "bright, cheerful and happy" mental attitude, and the outward manifestation of the same, is a magnet of success to the salesman. The "grouch" is the negative pole of personality, and does more to repel people than almost any other quality. So much in demand is the cheerful demeanor and mental state, that people often give undue preference to those possessing it, and pass over a "grouchy" individual of merit in favor of the man of less merit but who possesses the "sunshine" in his personality. The "man with the southern exposure" is in demand. There is enough in the world to depress people without having gloom thrust upon them by persons calling to sell goods. Well has the poet said:

"Laugh, and the world laughs with you;
Weep, and you weep alone.
For this sad old earth is in need of mirth;
It has troubles enough of its own."

The world prefers "Happy Jim" to "Gloomy Gus," and will bestow its favors upon the first while turning a cold shoulder to the second. The Human Wet Blanket is not a welcome guest, while the individual who manages to "let a little sunshine in" upon all occasions is always welcome. The optimistic and cheerful spirit creates for itself an atmosphere which, perhaps unconsciously, diffuses itself in all places visited by the individual. Cheerfulness is contagious, and is a most valuable asset. We have known individuals whose sunny exteriors caused a relief in the tension on the part of those whom they visited. We have heard it said of such people: "I am always glad to see that fellow—he brightens me up." This does not mean that one should endeavor to become a professional wit, a clown, or a comedian—that is not the point. The idea underlying this mental state and attribute of personality is *Cheerfulness*, and a disposition to look on the bright side of things, and to manifest that mental state as the sun does its rays. Learn to radiate Cheerfulness. It is not so much a matter of saying things, as it is a matter of thinking them. A man's inner thoughts are reflected in his outward personality.

So cultivate the inner *Cheerfulness* before you can hope to manifest its outer characteristics. There is nothing so pitiful, or which falls so flat, as a counterfeit Cheerfulness—it is worse than the minstrel jokes of the last decade. To be cheerful one does not have to be a "funny man." The atmosphere of true Cheerfulness can proceed only from within. The higher- class Japanese instruct their children to maintain a cheerful demeanor and a smiling face no matter what happens, even though the heart is breaking. They consider this the obligation of their caste, and regard it as most unworthy of the person, as well as insulting to others, to manifest any other demeanor or expression. Their theory, which forms a part of their wonderful code called "Bushido," is that it is an impertinence to obtrude one's grief, sorrow, misfortunes, or "grouch," upon others. They reserve for their own inner circle their sorrows and pains, and always present a cheerful and bright appearance to others. The Salesman would do well to remember the "Bushido,"—he needs it in his business. Avoid the "grouch" mental state as you would a pestilence. Don't be a "knocker"—for "knocks," like chickens, come home to roost, bringing their chicks with them.

IV. *Politeness.* Courtesy is a valuable asset to a Salesman. Not only this, but it is a trait characteristic of *gentlemen* in all walks of life, and is a duty toward oneself as well as toward others. By politeness and courtesy we do not mean the formal, artificial outward acts and remarks which are but the counterfeit of the real thing, but, instead, that respectful demeanor toward others which is the mark of innate refinement and good-breeding. Courtesy and politeness do not necessarily consist of formal rules of etiquette, but of an inner sympathy and understanding of others which manifests in a courteous demeanor toward them. Everyone likes to be treated with appreciation and understanding and is willing to repay the same in like form. One does not need to be a raw "jollier" in order to be polite. Politeness—true politeness—comes from within, and it is almost impossible to imitate it successfully. Its spirit may be expressed by the idea of trying to see the good in everyone and then acting toward the person as if his good were in plain evidence. Give to those with whom you come in contact the manner, attention and respect to which they would be entitled if they were actually manifesting the highest good within them.

One of the best retail salesmen we ever knew attributed his success to his ability to "get on the customer's side of the counter," that is, to try to see the matter from the customer's viewpoint. This led to a sympathetic understanding which was most valuable. If the Salesman can manage to put himself in the place of the customer, he may see things with a new light, and thus gain an understanding of the customer which will enable him, the Salesman, to manifest a true politeness toward his customers. But politeness and courtesy does not mean a groveling, cringing attitude of mind or demeanor. True politeness and courtesy must have as its background and support, Self Respect.

Allied to politeness is the quality called Tact, which is defined as the "peculiar skill or adroitness in doing or saying exactly that which is required by, or is suited to, the circumstances; nice perception or discernment." A little consideration will show that Tact must depend upon an understanding of the viewpoint and mental attitude of the other person, so that if one has the key to the one he may open the door of the other. An understanding of the other person's position, and an application of the true spirit of politeness, will go a long way toward establishing the quality of tactfulness. Tact is a queer combination of Worldly Wisdom and the Golden Rule—a mixture of the ability to seek into the other person's mind, and the ability to speak unto others as you would that others speak unto you, under the same circumstances. The trait called Adaptability, or the faculty of adjusting oneself to conditions, and to the personality of others, also belongs to this category. Adaptability depends upon the ability to see the other person's position. As a writer says: "Those individuals who are out of harmony with their surroundings disappear to make room for those who are in harmony with them." When the keynote of the understanding of the minds of others is found, the whole subject of true politeness, tact and adaptability is understood and may be applied in practice.

V. *Human Nature.* Closely allied to the subject of the preceding paragraphs, is that of Human Nature. A knowledge of Human Nature is very important to the Salesman. In order to understand the workings of the minds of others, one must not only understand the general psychological principles involved, but also the special manifestations of those principles. Nature tends to form classes and species, and the majority of people may be grouped into special classes depending upon their temperaments. An intelligent study of The New Psychology and the general subject of Human Nature in works on Physiognomy, etc., will do much to start one well upon the road to an understanding of Human Nature. But, after all, the best knowledge comes only when the general principles are tested and applied under observation in general experience.

In this particular work we have much to say upon certain features of Human Nature—in fact, as we have said, Human Nature is but Psychology. The following advice, from the pen of Prof. Fowler, the well known authority on Phrenology, is recommended to all Salesmen desirous of acquiring the faculty of understanding Human Nature: "Scan closely all the actions of men, with a view to ascertain their motives and mainsprings of action; look with a sharp eye at man, woman, child, all you meet, as if you would read them through; note particularly the expression of the eye, as if you would imbibe what it signifies; say to yourself: What faculty prompted this expression or that action; drink in the general looks, attitude, natural language, and manifestation of the man, and yield yourself to the impressions naturally made on you—that is, study human nature both as a philosophy and as a sentiment, or as if being impressed thereby."

A forthcoming volume of this series, to be entitled "Human Nature," will go into this subject in detail.

CHAPTER 3

THE MIND OF THE SALESMAN (CONTINUED)

VI. *Hope.* The Salesman should cultivate the Optimistic Outlook upon Life. He should encourage the earnest expectation of the good things to come, and move forward to the realization thereof. Much of life success depends upon the mental attitude of, and the confident expectation of, a successful outcome. Earnest Desire, Confident Expectation, and Resolute Action—this is the threefold key of attainment. Thought manifests itself in action, and we grow in accordance with the mental pattern or mould we create for ourselves. If you will look around you you will find that the men who have succeeded, and who are succeeding, are those who have maintained the hopeful mental attitude—who have always looked forward to the star of hope even in the moments of the greatest trouble and temporary reverses. If a man loses his hope permanently he is defeated. Hope is the incentive which is always drawing man onward and upward. Hope backed by Will and Determination is almost invincible. Learn to look on the bright side of things, to believe in your ultimate success. Learn to look upward and forward—heed the motto, "look aloft!" Cultivate the "rubber-ball spirit," by which you will be able to bounce higher up the harder you are thrown down. There is a subtle psychological law by the operation of which we tend to materialize our ideals. The "confident expectation" backed by actions will win out in the end. Hitch your wagon to the Star of Hope.

VII. *Enthusiasm.* Very few people understand the true meaning of the word "enthusiasm," although they may use it quite frequently in ordinary conversation. Enthusiasm means far more than energy, activity, interest and hope—it means the expression of the "soul" in mental and physical actions. The Greeks used the word as meaning "inspiration; moved by the gods," from which arose the later meaning of "inspired by a superhuman or divine power." The modern usage is defined as: "Enkindled and kindling fervor of the soul; ardent and imaginative zeal or interest; lively manifestation of joy or zeal;" etc. A person filled with enthusiasm seems to move and act from the very centre of his being—that part which we mean when we say "soul." There is a wonderful power in rightly directed enthusiasm, which serves not only to arouse within one his full powers, but also tends to impress others in the direction of mental contagion. Mental states are contagious, and enthusiasm is one of the most active of mental states. Enthusiasm comes nearer to being "soul-power" than any other outward expression of mental states. It is allied to the soul-stirring impulse of music, poetry, and the drama. We can *feel* it in the words of a writer, speaker, orator, preacher, singer or poet. Enthusiasm may be analyzed as Inspired Interest. As Walter D. Moody says: "It will be found that all men possessed of personal magnetism are very much in earnest. Their intense earnestness is magnetic." The best authorities agree that Enthusiasm is the active principle of what has been called Personal Magnetism.

An old writer has well said: "All of us emit a sphere, aura, or halo, impregnated with the very essence of ourselves, sensitives know it, so do our dogs and other pets; so does a hungry lion or tiger; aye, even flies, snakes and insects, as we know to our cost. Some of us are magnetic—others not. Some of us are warm, attractive, love-inspiring and friendship-making, while others are cold, intellectual, thoughtful, reasoning, but not magnetic. Let a learned man of the latter type address an audience and it will soon tire of his intellectual discourse, and will manifest symptoms of drowsiness. He talks at them, but not into them—he makes them think, not feel, which is most tiresome to the majority of persons, and few speakers succeed who attempt to merely make people think—they want to be made to feel. People will pay liberally to be made to feel or laugh, while they will begrudge a dime for instruction or talk that will make them think. Pitted against a learned man of the type mentioned above, let there be a half-educated, but very loving, ripe and mellow man, with but nine-tenths of the logic and erudition of the first man, yet such a man carries along his crowd with perfect ease, and everybody is wide-awake, treasuring up every good thing that falls from his lips. The reasons are palpable and plain. It is heart against head; soul against logic; and soul is bound to win every time." And as Newman says: "Deductions have no power of persuasion. The heart is commonly reached, not through the reason, but through the imagination, by means of direct impressions, by the testimony of facts and events, by history, by description. Persons influence us, looks subdue us, deeds inflame us." Enthusiasm imparts that peculiar quality that we call "*life*," which constitutes such an important part in the personality of a salesman. Remember we have analyzed enthusiasm as *inspired earnestness*—think over this analysis, and grasp its inner meaning. The very word "ENTHUSIASM" is inspiring—visualize it and let it incite you to its expression when you feel "dead." The very thought of it is a stimulant!

VIII. *Determination.* The Salesman needs the quality of dogged determination, persistence, and "stick-to-itiveness." This bulldog quality must be developed. The "I Can and I Will" spirit must be cultivated. Determination is composed of several constituent faculties. First comes Combativeness or the quality of "tackling" obstacles. This is a marked quality in all strong characters. It manifests as courage, boldness, resistance, opposition, and disposition to combat opposition rather than to yield to it.

Allied to this faculty is another which bears the very inadequate name of Destructiveness, which expresses itself in the direction of breaking down barriers, pushing aside obstacles, making headway; pushing to the front; holding one's own; etc. It is the quality of the man who makes his own paths and builds up his own trade. It is the "pioneer" faculty of the mind which clears away the ground, lays foundations and builds the first log-cabin.

Then comes Continuity, the faculty which is well-defined as "stick-to- itiveness," which enables one to stick to his task until it is finished. This faculty gives stability and staying qualities, and enables a man to *finish* well. The lack of this quality often neutralizes the work of other good faculties, causing the person to "let go" too soon, and to thus lose the fruits of his labors.

Finally, comes the faculty of Firmness, which gives to one the quality of tenacity, perseverance, fixity, decision and stability, accompanied by a certain "stubborn tendency" which holds the other faculties together. A certain amount of this quality of "jackass courage" is needed in the mental make up of a Salesman. If a person is 'set' to a certain extent it enables him to maintain his position without the constant wear and tear upon his will that is met with by those lacking it. This faculty prevents one from being "sidetracked," and enables him to "put his hand to the plow and look not backward." It holds the chisel of the will up against the metal of circumstances until the work is accomplished. It enables one to be like the rock against which harmlessly beat the waves of opposition and competition. It enables one to see his object, and then to march straight to it.

IX. *Secretiveness.* We mention this quality, not because it is one which plays such an important part in the world of Salesmanship, but because the tendency of the average Salesman is to talk too freely regarding matters which should be kept to himself. This failing on the part of the Salesman is due to the free expression which his work necessitates. He should remember, however, that many a good plan has miscarried by reason of the tendency of the Salesman to "blab," or to "give away" his hopes, plans and expectations. The Salesman should think thrice before speaking regarding any matter of office or personal policy, plans, methods, or other things which he would not like his competitors to know. It is a safe rule, laid down by a very successful business man, that one should "Never speak of anything that he is not desirous of his principal competitor hearing—for hear it he will if one speaks of it." The world is full of the "little birds" who delight in carrying tales—the "walls have ears" with microphone, wireless telegraphic attachments. Be a diplomat in matters of the kind to which we have referred. A little thought should convince that if you *yourself* do not respect your own secrets, you can not expect others to do so.

X. *Acquisitiveness.* This faculty manifests as the desire for acquiring things; gaining; possessing; reaching out for; etc. It is often condemned by people, because of the unpleasant traits manifested by those in whom it is abnormally developed, as the miser, the "hog," and the "stingy" person. But it is not well to hastily condemn this faculty, for without it we would become desireless, spendthrift, wasteful, without resources, and poor. The man who would succeed in any line of business must cultivate Acquisitiveness, if he is deficient in it. He must learn to want and earnestly desire the good things of life, and to reach out for them. He must desire to accumulate something for himself, for by so doing he will work so that he will make a valuable accumulating channel for his employers. Acquisitiveness is one of the animating principles of the business world, evade it though we may try to. It is hypocritical to deny this. The facts are too plain to be brushed aside or denied. As the writer has said in another work: "People are all after money—every blessed mother's son and daughter of them—in one way or another." What is the use of denying it. Some day we may have better economic conditions—I pray to God that we may—but until that time all of us must chase the nimble dollar to the best of our ability. For unless a man does this thing, then shall he not eat; nor be clothed; nor have shelter; nor books; nor music; nor anything else that makes life worth living for one who thinks and feels. It seems to me the proper balance is preserved in the following statement: "While you're getting, get all you can—*but give the other fellow a chance.*"

XI. *Approbativeness.* This is the quality which manifests in a desire for praise, flatter, approval, fame, etc. The average Salesman does not need to develop this faculty—his temperament is very apt to make him have it too highly developed. It is all very well to feel a certain pleasure from the approval of others of work well done. But it is a decided weakness for one to be so sensitive to the opinions of others that they suffer from their disapproval, or from the lack of praise. He who is dependent upon the praise of the crowd, or the approval of the mob is a fool, deserving of pity. The crowd is fickle and tomorrow may turn on those whom they are praising to- day. Moreover there is always much secret envy and jealousy mixed with the praise of others.

Did you ever notice how eagerly people relate the slip-up or stumble of those whom they have been praising? Be not deceived by the plaudits of the crowd. Nor should you allow yourself to be deterred from a right course because of fear of blame. Learn to rely on what you, yourself, know to be right. "Be sure you're right, then go ahead." Learn to stand upon your own feet, and do not lean upon others. Shake the crowd off your heels—mind your own business and let others do likewise. And look the world squarely in the eye while you are talking to it, too. It will understand you, if you do not truckle to it. But never cringe to it—else it will rend you to pieces. "They say; what do they say; let them say!" "Do not worry about it—your friends will not care, and your enemies will criticise anyway; so what's the use?" Say to yourself: "I am the Captain of my Soul." And remember Burton's glorious words of freedom and courage:

> "Do what thy manhood bids thee do, from none but self expect applause;
> He noblest lives and noblest dies who makes and keeps his self-made laws.
> All other Life is living Death, a world where none but Phantoms dwell.
> A breath, a wind, a sound, a voice, a tinkling of the Camel's bell."

The difference between Egoism and Egotism consists largely of the difference between Self-Respect and Approbativeness. Develop the first, and restrain the second—if you wish to become an Individual. And the successful Salesman is always an Individual—standing out from and above the crowd of the "mere persons" or "order-takers." Be a Man, and not a human looking glass reflecting the ideas, opinions, and wishes of all those around you. Be creative, not imitative. Flattery is the food for apes, not for men.

Personal Expression. While one's personal expression in the direction of clothing, walk, voice, etc., can scarcely be called mental qualities, yet they must be considered as *expressions* of mental qualities—outward manifestations of inward states. So true is this that people naturally judge one's character by these outward expressions. And, moreover, there is a subtle reaction of one's outward manifestations upon one's mental states. One's walk, carriage and demeanor influence one's mental attitude, as we may prove by changing these outward manifestations and noting our changed feelings. As someone has said: "The consciousness of being well dressed imparts a certain serenity and peace which even religion sometimes fails to give us."

And, as for physical attitudes, etc., hear what several eminent psychologists tell us. Prof. Halleck says: "By inducing an expression we can often cause its allied emotion." Prof. James says: "Whistling to keep up courage is no mere figure of speech. On the other hand, sit all day in a moping posture, sigh, and reply to everything with a dismal voice, and your melancholy lingers. There is no more valuable precept in moral education than this: If we wish to conquer undesirable emotional tendencies in ourselves we must assiduously, and in the first instance cold-bloodedly, go through the *outward movements*, of those contrary dispositions which we wish to cultivate. Smooth the brow, brighten the eye, contract the dorsal rather than the ventral aspect of the frame, and speak in a major key, pass the genial compliment and your heart must indeed be frigid if it does not gradually thaw."

Dr. Woods Hutchinson says: "To what extent muscular contractions condition emotions, as Prof. James has suggested, may be easily tested by a quaint and simple little experiment upon a group of the smallest voluntary muscles of the body, those that move the eyeball. Choose some time when you are sitting quietly in your room, free from all disturbing thoughts and influences. Then stand up, and assuming an easy position, cast the eyes upward, and hold them in that position for thirty seconds. Instantly and involuntarily you will be conscious of a tendency toward reverential, devotional, contemplative ideas and thoughts. Then turn the eyes sideways, glancing directly to the right or to the left, through half-closed lids. Within thirty seconds images of suspicion, of uneasiness, or of dislike will rise unbidden to the mind. Turn the eyes on one side and slightly downward, and suggestions of jealousy or coquetry will be apt to spring unbidden. Direct your gaze downward toward the floor, and you are likely to go off into a fit of reverie or abstraction." Maudsley says: "The specific muscular action is not merely an exponent of passion, but truly an essential part of it. If we try while the features are fixed in the expression of one passion to call up in the mind a different one, we shall find it impossible to do so."

In view of the above statements, we may readily see the importance of cultivating those outward expressions which are co-related to desirable mental states or feelings. By so doing we arouse in our minds those particular states or feelings. And, moreover, we tend to impress others with the possession on our part of the co-related mental qualities. One's outward expression is a powerful instrument of suggestion to others, and people are unconsciously and instinctively affected by it, to our benefit or detriment. Let us therefore consider, briefly, the general principles underlying personal expression along the lines indicated.

Carriage and Walk. In the first part of the previous chapter, under the sub- head of "Self-Respect" we have given you the advice of a good authority concerning the proper carriage. The key is: Carry yourself in a manner showing your Self-Respect, Poise, and Consideration of Others. Another authority gives the following directions for the correct position in standing: "(1) Heels together; (2) head up, with chin slightly drawn in rather than protruding; (3) eyes front; (4) shoulders thrown back but not elevated; (5) chest expanded; (6) abdomen slightly drawn in, and not allowed to protrude; (7) arms dropped naturally to the sides, with the little fingers lightly touching the sides of the thigh. This may make you feel a little stiff and awkward at first, but, if you persevere, will soon establish itself as second nature with you."

Another authority says: "The easiest way in which to acquire a correct carriage is to imagine that you are suspended from on high with a line, the lowest end of the line being fastened to the lower end of your breast-bone. If you will stand and walk as if you are so suspended, the result will be that you will acquire an easy, graceful, gliding walk, and a correct carriage and natural position." Another authority gives the following advice: "The following method if observed in walking and standing, will impart a desirable physical poise and will keep you erect and in a graceful attitude while walking: Stand with your back toward the wall, with the heels, legs, hips, shoulders and back of head touching the wall, and with the chin slightly drawn in. Press up against the wall firmly. You will find yourself in an uncomfortable position, and one that is unnatural and incorrect. Then, keeping your heels to the wall, allow your body to swing forward into a natural position, being careful to keep the body firm in the same 'form,' avoiding relaxation, swinging yourself forward from the ankle joints alone. When you find that the correct poised, natural position has been attained, hold it, and march forward in what will be the natural, normal, well-balanced walking position. Practice this repeatedly, several times every day, until you have fully acquired the habit."

Shaking Hands. When you grasp another's hand in the act of "shaking hands," do not do so in a listless, cold-blooded manner—do not extend to the other man a flabby, clammy, fish-like hand. But take hold of his hand as if you liked to do it—throw interest into the proceeding. More than this—throw feeling into it. Throw into the hand-clasp the feeling: "*I like you, and you like me*." Then, when you draw your hand away, if possible let your fingers slide over the palm of his hand in a caressing manner, allowing his first finger to pass between your thumb and forefinger, close up in the crotch of the thumb. Practice this well, until you can perform it without thinking of it. You will find merit in the method. Grasp the other person's hand "as if he were your best girl's millionaire father-in-law."

Voice. The Salesman should cultivate a voice with expression in it. His voice should convey his belief in what he is saying, and his interest in the story. You will find it an aid in this direction if you will learn to visualize your thoughts—that is, to make a mental picture of the thing you are saying. One can always describe better that which they see before them. In the degree that you can see your mental picture, so will be your degree of power in expressing it to another in words, and so will be the degree of feeling in your tone. The voice should express the meaning of your thought rather than being merely the symbol of it. Try to say "Good Morning" as if you meant it—then say it in the usual way. Do you see the difference? Throw your thought and feeling into your voice. Forget all about yourself and the other man and concentrate your thought and feeling into your voice.

Many people make the mistake of "speaking with their muscles instead of with their nerves." They throw muscular energy into their words, when they should use nervous energy, or thought-force. The former has but little effect on the mind of the other, while the second vibrates subtly and reaches the feelings of those addressed. *Feel*, when you wish to speak impressively, and your tones will reflect the same, and induce a similar feeling in others. It is a point worth remembering that one may "bring down" the voice of an excited person to one's own pitch, if the latter is firmly held at the customary pitch, in a firm manner. Not only does this "bring down" the other man's voice, but his feelings will also follow suit, and besides, you also manage to keep your own temper and poise. Never raise your voice because another raises his—resist the tendency, and maintain your poise and power by so doing. This is worth remembering.

The Eyes. Learn to look people in the eyes when you are speaking to them. Not in a staring manner, but firmly, politely and easily. This may be acquired with a little practice. Practice on yourself in the mirror if you prefer. A shifting, restless gaze produces a bad impression, while a firm, honest gaze will incline people in your favor. You will find that strong men—men who influence others—almost always have a firm, strong gaze. It is worth practice, work and time, to acquire this personal trait.

Clothes. A man is very often known by his clothes, or at least judged by them. The Salesman should pay attention to this point of personal expression, since it will count much for or against him. The first point to remember is that *cleanliness* is the first requisite in clothing. Keep your clothes clean and well pressed. Particularly keep your linen clean, for nothing in the way of dress acts so much against a man as soiled linen. Another important point is to keep the extremities well clad—that is, the head, feet and hands. A soiled or worn hat; a soiled or frayed collar; an old, or unpolished pair of shoes; ragged sleeves or frayed cuffs—these things are more easily noticed and count more against a man than a shabby suit. Better an old suit well brushed, with a good hat, shoes and clean cuffs—than the reverse.

One should always wear as good clothes as his means will permit, and such as will be in keeping with his occupation and position. The rule is to get as good material as possible, and cut reasonably within the prevailing style—but avoiding all extremes, or fanciful designs. *A well-dressed business man should give neither the appearance of shabbiness nor of being "dressed-up."* He should present the appearance of general neatness without attracting any special attention to his clothing. When a man's clothes specially attract one, that man is not well dressed, but either poorly dressed or over-dressed. The "happy mean" between the two extremes is to be sought after. Polonius' advice to his son is well worth memorizing: "Costly thy habit as thy purse can buy, but not expressed in fancy; rich, not gaudy; for the apparel oft proclaims the man."

Details of Appearance. Personal cleanliness and neatness are pre-requisites of the Salesman who wishes to produce a favorable impression. There is nothing that will so tend to prejudice the average business man against a new caller as the appearance of neglect of personal care. The body should be well- bathed; the hair trimmed and neatly brushed; the face cleanly shaven; the teeth well brushed; the nails clean; the shoes polished; the necktie and collar clean; the clothes brushed. Avoid the smell of liquor or tobacco on the breath, and eschew as fatal the odor of strong perfumery on the clothes or handkerchief. The yellow stains of the cigarette showing on the fingers, and the disgusting odor attaching to the cigarette habit, have lost many a man a favorable bearing. The cigarette is "taboo" to many men who smoke other forms of tobacco. These things are instinctively recognized by the buyer as manifestations of the mind of the salesman—a part of his personality—and very rightly so, for if the mind be kept above them they do not manifest. All these things go toward forming the impression which one person always makes upon another at the first meeting, and which have so much to do with securing a favorable notice during the Approach of the Salesman.

CHAPTER 4

THE MIND OF THE BUYER

The second important element in a sale is the Mind of the Buyer. In the mind of the buyer is fought the battle of the sale. Within its boundaries are manifested the movements which win or lose the day. As a writer on the subject has said: "The buyer's brain is the board upon which the game is played. The faculties of the brain are the men. The salesman moves or guides these faculties as he would chess men or checkers on a board." In order to understand the ground upon which your battle must be fought, and the mental elements which you must combat, persuade, move, push or attract, you must understand the various faculties of the mind, as well as the mind as a whole. Let us, therefore, consider the various mental faculties which are employed actively by a buyer in the mental process of a purchase.

I. *Quality.* In the first place, let us consider that which the phrenologists call "Quality," by which they express the various degrees of fineness or coarseness in a man's mental make-up which is usually indicated by his appearance and physical characteristics. This "quality" in a man is akin to what we call "class," "breeding," or "blood" in the higher animals. It is difficult to explain, but is universally recognized. At one extreme of "quality" we find those individuals who are fine-grained, refined, high-strung, intense, and inclined to be susceptible to emotional or sentimental influence, poetry, music, etc., and are apt to be more or less impractical and out of harmony with the material world of men and affairs. At the other extreme we find those individuals who are coarse-grained, of coarse and unrefined tastes, animal, gross, unrefined, and generally "swinish." Between these two extremes we find many degrees in the scale. The outward physical signs of the person, such as the coarseness or fineness of his skin, hair, nails, ears and facial features, as well as his general form and characteristics, will usually give the careful observer the key to the degree of a man's "quality." It will be well for the Salesman to acquaint himself with these characteristics, for they throw much light on the general character of people.

Next in order come what are called the Temperaments, by which term phrenologists designate the general classes into which individuals fit. As a rule, however, an individual manifests the elements of several of the temperaments—that is, they blend in him. The best phrenological authorities classify the temperaments as follows: (1) The Vital; (2) The Motive; (3) The Mental; the characteristics of which are described as follows:

The Vital Temperament. This temperament is indicated by a predominance of the purely physical or "animal" propensities. Those in whom it predominates are distinguished by a round head, wide space between the corners of the eyes and the ears, side-head full, broad forehead (not necessarily high). They are generally fleshy with a "well-fed" appearance, inclined to be broad shouldered and deep chested and with a "bull neck"—splendid animals, in fact. Their mental characteristics are love of eating and drinking, and animal comforts; impulsiveness, impetuosity, heartiness, quick temper, zeal and ardor, often shrewd and cunning but without great depth, susceptible to flattery and appeal to selfish emotions and prejudices, and loving pleasure. They are generally selfish and grasping toward that which caters to their pleasure and physical welfare. Try to "get all that is coming to them," and yet at the same time tend toward conviviality and are desirous of being thought "good fellows." Are usually excitable, and are easily thrown off their balance. Those in whom this temperament is deficient manifest physical characteristics opposite to those above mentioned, and are more or less anaemic, or bloodless, and show a lack of vitality and physical well-being. Those in whom this temperament predominates make good butchers, hotel- keepers, captains, locomotive engineers, traders, politicians, contractors, etc. They are reached through their feelings rather than through their intellect.

The Motive Temperament. This temperament is indicated by a predominance of muscular strength, endurance, toughness, and powers of action. Those in whom it predominates are distinguished by a general leanness and spareness; strongly marked and prominent features, usually with a large nose and high cheek bones; large and strong teeth; large joints and knuckles—the Abraham Lincoln physical characteristics, in fact. Their mental characteristics are determination, persistence, combativeness, destructiveness, endurance, thoroughness, management, executive ability, creative power, stubbornness, powers of resistance, and often an indomitable spirit. Their emotions are not on the surface, but when once aroused are strong and persistent. They are slow to wrath, but are good fighters and will stay to the finish. They are generally canny and shrewd, instinctively. They are the active and persistent workers of the world. It is this temperament in one which supplies his motive power—his ability and taste for work. Those in whom this temperament is deficient manifest physical characteristics opposite to those above mentioned, and accordingly are averse to work or exertion of any kind.

The Mental Temperament. This temperament is indicated by a predominance of nervous force, mental activity, reasoning power, imagination, and a brain development rather than bodily strength or physical activity. Those in whom it predominates are distinguished by a slight build, small bones and muscles, general fineness of structure, quick motions, signs of nervous energy, sharp features, thin lips, thin, finely shaped, and often pointed nose, high forehead, and expressive eyes. Their mental characteristics are activity in reasoning processes, active imagination, susceptibility to disturbance from uncongenial environment and distasteful company, love of mental activity and often a distaste for physical activity, sensitiveness, extremes of feeling and emotion, eager and enthusiastic, and the general traits popularly designated as "temperamental." Those in whom this temperament is deficient manifest characteristics opposite to those above mentioned, and are averse to mental activity.

Blended Temperaments. Nearly every individual possesses the three temperaments blended in various proportions and combinations. In some, one temperament predominates largely and gives us the distinctive characteristics of that class. But in others, often two temperaments will predominate, leaving the third scarcely manifest. In others, the three are so well blended and balanced that the individual is known as "well balanced" temperamentally—this being considered the ideal condition.

Prof. Fowler, one of the old authorities in phrenology, says of the blended temperaments: "Excessive Motive with deficient Mental gives power and sluggishness, so that the talents lie dormant. Excessive Vital gives physical power and enjoyment, but too little of the mental and moral, along with coarseness and animality. Excessive Mental confers too much mind for body, too much sentimentalism and exquisiteness, along with greenhouse precocity. Whereas their equal balance gives an abundant supply of vital energy, physical stamina, and mental power and susceptibility. They may be compared to the several parts of a steamboat and its appurtenances. The Vital is the steampower; the Motive, the hulk or frame-work; the Mental, the freight and passengers. The Vital predominating, generates more animal energy than can well be worked off, and causes restlessness, excessive passion, and a pressure which endangers outbursts and overt actions; predominant Motive gives too much frame or hulk; moves slowly, and with weak Mental is too light freighted to secure the great ends of life; predominant Mental overloads, and endangers sinking; but all equally balanced and powerful, carry great loads rapidly and well, and accomplish wonders. Such persons unite cool judgment with intense and well governed feelings; great force of character and intellect with perfect consistency; scholarship with sound common sense; far seeing sagacity with brilliancy; and have the highest order of both physiology and mentality."

The Salesman should thoroughly acquaint himself with the characteristics of each of the three temperaments, and should also learn to analyze them when found blended and in combination. An understanding of a man's temperament will often give one the key to his general character and disposition, which will be of the greatest advantage to the Salesman. Many students of human nature devote their entire attention to a study of the several faculties of the mind, ignoring the force and effect of the temperaments. We consider this to be a mistake, for a thorough knowledge of the temperaments gives one a general key to character, and, as a fact, it is generally found that given a certain temperament or combination of the same, a good phrenologist will be able to indicate just what faculties are apt to be found in the ascendency in such a character. And as the average Salesman cannot spare the time to become an expert phrenologist, it will be seen that a correct knowledge of the temperaments gives him his best working knowledge of the subject of character reading.

Let us now consider the various groups of mental faculties which are manifested by the buyer in his business, and which should be understood by the Salesman in order that he may successfully meet the impulses arising therefrom in the mind of the buyer. Our consideration of these groups of faculties must necessarily be brief, but we shall include the essential features.

The Social Faculties. This group of faculties includes *Amativeness* or Sexuality; *Conjugality* or Marital Inclination; *Parental Love* or Love of Offspring; *Friendship* or Love of Companionship; *Inhabitiveness* or Love of Home. Phrenology teaches that this group of organs occupies the lower back portion of the head, giving the appearance of bulging behind the ears. *Amativeness* or Sexuality when highly developed causes one to be at the mercy of the attraction of the opposite sex. While normally developed it plays a worthy part in life, its excessive development manifests in licentiousness, and when deficient manifests in an aversion to the opposite sex or a coldness and reserve. Persons in whom this faculty is in excess will neglect business for sex attraction, and will allow themselves to be "sidetracked" by reason thereof. In selling a man of this kind, keep him away from this particular subject, or he will not give you his attention. *Conjugality* or Marital Inclination when highly developed causes one to be largely influenced by one's companion in marriage. A man of this kind will be largely governed by his wife's wishes, tastes and desires, consequently if his wife "says so" the battle is won. Some men, however, while having Amativeness largely developed, have but small Conjugality, and if one love is not found satisfactory, another is substituted—an "affinity" takes the wife's place. *Parental Love* or Love of Offspring when highly developed causes one to idolize his children and to be capable of influence through them. Such men are prone to relate anecdotes regarding their children and to bore listeners with recitals of infantile brightness and precocity. They generally have photographs of their children about their desks. An appeal to the interests of the children always reaches the attention and interest of these people. *Friendship*, or Love of Companionship, when highly developed causes one to seek society, form attachments of friendship, enjoy social pleasures, do favors for those whom they like, enjoy entertaining and being entertained. Such a man will be more apt to base his business dealings upon likes and acquaintance rather than upon reason or judgment, and are comparatively easily persuaded by those whom they like. An appearance of sociability generally attracts them to those manifesting it. The quality of "good fellowship" appeals to this class. *Inhabitiveness* or Love of Home when highly developed causes one to become *attached to places*, localities and associations. Such a man will be full of patriotism, local pride and prejudice and provincialism. He will resent any apparent "slur" upon his locality, and will appreciate any favorable comment on his home place and locality. These people are like cats who are attached to places rather than to people. Their township is usually their idea of "my country."

The Selfish Faculties. This group of faculties includes *Vitativeness*, or Love of Life; *Combativeness*, or Love of Opposing; *Destructiveness*, or Love of Breaking Through; *Alimentiveness*, or Love of Appetite; *Bibativeness*, or Love of Drink; *Acquisitiveness*, or Love of Gain; *Secretiveness*, or Cunning; *Cautiousness*, or Prudence; *Approbativeness*, or Love of Praise; *Self Esteem*, or Self Reliance. Phrenology teaches that this group of organs occupy the sides of the back part of the head. *Vitativeness*, or Love of Life, when highly developed causes one to manifest a determination to live, and a great fear of death. Anything promising increased health or long life will greatly attract these people, and anything arousing a fear of ill health or death will influence them greatly. These people are excellent customers for health appliances, books on health, etc. *Combativeness*, or Love of Opposing, when highly developed causes one to desire a "scrap" or an argument or debate. These people can best be handled by seemingly allowing them to win in argument, and then leading them to suggest the thing that the Salesman has had in his mind all the time. These people may be led, or coaxed, but never driven. With them it is always a case of "sugar catches more flies than vinegar," or of the hot sun causing the man to drop the cloak which the fierce north wind was unable to blow away from him. A man of this kind will be so pleased at beating another in an argument on a minor point, that he will forget the main point and will be in a humor to be persuaded. Always avoid a direct argument or dispute with these people on important points—they will let their pride of combat obscure their judgment. But they will be ready to bestow favors on those whom they believe they have worsted in argument. *Destructiveness*, or Love of Breaking Through, when highly developed causes one to take great pleasure in doing things in new ways; in breaking precedents and defying authority, and in breaking down obstacles. If you can arouse this spirit in such a man, by showing him how he may do these things with your goods, he will fall in line. A man of this kind may be interested at once in any proposition whereby he may be enabled to do something in a novel way here—to defy opposition or established custom—or to break down opposing obstacles. The keynote of this faculty is: "Make Way." *Alimentiveness*, or Love of Appetite, when highly developed causes one to incline toward gluttony and gormandizing, and to place undue importance upon the pleasures of the table. A man of this kind "lives to eat" instead of "eating to live," and may be reached through his weakest point—his stomach. To such a man a good dinner is more convincing than a logical argument. *Bibativeness*, or Love of Drink, when highly developed causes one to manifest an inordinate taste for liquids of all kinds. In some cases, where alcoholic drinks are avoided by such people, they will run to excess in the direction of "soft drinks" such as ginger ale, soda water, etc. It does not follow that these people are fond of the effects of alcohol, the craving seemingly being for liquids in some form. Such people, if their appetites are not controlled, will let their taste for drinks run away with their judgment and reason.

Acquisitiveness, or Love of Gain, when highly developed causes one to be very grasping, avaricious, and often miserly. But, when not so highly developed, it causes one to manifest a keen trading instinct, and is a necessary factor in the mental make-up of the successful merchant. Those in whom it is highly developed will be interested in any proposition which seems to them to promise gain or saving. In selling such a man, the effort should be to keep the one point of *profit or saving* always in evidence. In some cases this faculty, too highly developed and not counterbalanced by other faculties, will make a man "penny wise and pound-foolish," and will focus his mental gaze so closely on the nickel held close to his eye that he will not see the dollar a little further off. The "money talk" is the only one that will appeal to these people.

Secretiveness, or Cunning, when highly developed causes one to incline toward double-dealing, duplicity, trickery and deception. It is the "foxy" faculty, which, while useful to a certain degree, becomes undesirable when carried to excess. In dealing with a man of this kind, be on guard so far as accepting his statements at full value is concerned. Accept his statements "with a grain of salt." Those who wish to "fight the devil with his own fire" can reach these people by allowing them to think that they are overreaching or getting the best of the Salesman. The Salesman who is apparently defeated by these people, is very apt to have discounted their methods in advance, and has mapped out his line of retreat in advance so that the defeat is really a victory. These people often will sacrifice a real advantage concerning a big thing for the sake of tricking one out of a small advantage. To trick another causes them to feel a glow of righteous well-being and self-satisfaction, and makes them forget the main point in the deal. A small victory thus won acts on them like the good dinner to the Alimentive man, or flattery to the Approbative person. A faculty developed to excess is always a weak point which can be used by others who understand it.

Cautiousness, or Prudence, while an admirable quality when normally developed, becomes, when highly developed, an undesirable quality. When highly developed it causes one to be over-anxious, fearful, afraid to act, liable to panic, etc. These people must be cultivated carefully, and led to acquire confidence and trust. One should be very careful in dealing with these people not to cause suspicion or alarm. They should be treated with the utmost fairness, and given full explanations of matters of which they are in doubt. As a rule they are very slow in giving confidence, but when they once place confidence in a person they are very apt to stick to him. Their very fearfulness acts to prevent their making changes when confidence is once secured. These people cannot be "rushed," as a rule—they require time in order to gain confidence. They are, however, subject to an occasional "rush" by reason of their panicky disposition, if they can be made to fear that if they do not act some competitor will be given the chance, or that prices will advance if they do not order at once. These people must be handled carefully, and the Salesman who masters their nature will be well repaid for his trouble and pains.

Approbativeness, or Love of Praise, when highly developed causes one to be susceptible to flattery, desirous of praise, fond of "showing off" and displaying himself, vain, sensitive to criticism, and generally egotistical and often pompous. This quality when highly developed is a weakness and gives to an adversary a powerful lever to work. The Salesman, while secretly detesting this quality in a buyer, nevertheless finds it a very easy channel of approach and weapon of success, when he once understands its characteristics. These people can be reached by an apparent "falling in" with their opinion of themselves, and a manifestation of the proper respect in manner and words. These are the people to whom the "soft soap" is applied liberally, and who are carried away by an apparent appreciation of their own excellence. They will be willing to bestow all sorts of favors upon those who are sufficiently able to "understand" them, and to perceive the existence of those superlative qualities which the cruel, cold, unfeeling world has ignored. These are the people for whom the word "jolly" was invented, and who are ready to absorb the available world-supply of that article.

Self Esteem, or Self Reliance, is a very different quality from that just described, although many people seem unable to make the distinction. Self Esteem when highly developed causes one to appreciate one's powers and qualities, while not blinding oneself to one's faults. It gives a sense of self- help, self-respect, self-reliance, dignity, complacency, and independence. Carried to an extreme it manifests as hauteur, superciliousness, imperiousness and tyranny. It is a characteristic of the majority of successful men who have made their own way by their own efforts. These people insist upon having their own way, and using their own minds—they resent apparent influence or suggestions, and often deliberately turn down a proposition simply because they think that an effort is being made to force them into it. The best way to deal with these people is to frankly acknowledge their right to think for themselves, both in your manner, tone and actions—and to present the proposition to them in an impersonal way, apparently leaving the whole matter to their own good judgment. A logical appeal appeals to them providing you do not make the mistake of pitting yourself against them as an opponent in argument. You may play the part of the lawyer to them, but remember always they want to play the part of judge, and not that of the opposing counsel. If a matter be subtly suggested to them in such a way as to make them think that they have thought it themselves, they will favor it. Always give them a chance to think out the point themselves—they like it. One need not cringe to or flatter these people. All that is necessary is to maintain your own self-respect, but at the same time let them walk a little ahead of you, or stand just a little bit higher—that is all they need to make them feel comfortable. They much prefer being a little higher or ahead of a strong man than a weakling—it is more complimentary to them. They appreciate the one who forces them to use their heaviest guns—but who finally allows them to claim the victory.

CHAPTER 5

THE MIND OF THE BUYER (CONTINUED)

The Faculties of Application. This group consists of two qualities: that of *Firmness*, or Decision; and that of *Continuity*, or Patience. These faculties, together with Self-Esteem, are located at the upper-back, or back-upper, part of the head.

Firmness, or Decision, when highly developed causes one to manifest stability, tenacity, fixedness of purpose, often reaching the point of obstinacy, mulishness and stubbornness. These people cannot be driven, or forced into anything. They are "mighty set" in their ways, and when they once take a position are very apt to stick to it "right or wrong." They are apt to fight to the last ditch for what they consider principle, and will hold on to the end in what they believe to be right. To attempt to drive them by force is to dash one's head against a stone wall. The only way to handle these people is to endeavor to get them interested in your side of the case before they have "set" their minds and made up their opinion. If they have already been prejudiced against your case, the only way is to give up the fight from the front, and endeavor to present the matter from a different viewpoint, or angle, so that new points will be presented which take the matter out of the old category. These people will never give in unless they can say: "Oh, that of course alters the matter entirely;" or "Oh, well, that places it in a new light;" or "That is an entirely different proposition," etc. Leave them victors of the positions upon which they are "set," and endeavor to enlist their interest upon some new aspects, points, or principles—you have at least an even chance of winning on the new point, whereas you have none whatever on the old one. If, however, you can fit your case to some of their established prejudices, for or against, you have won your battle, for their quality of stability will then be employed in your favor instead of against it. You will have to fit your case to their moulds—cut your garment according to their pattern. A stubborn and balky horse or mule can often be started in motion by turning its attention to a new thing—such as putting a piece of twisted paper in its ear, adjusting its harness in a new way, etc. The same principle will work on stubborn men, "set" in their ways. Get their mind off the point in question, and they will be rational. Let them have their own way about their own points—and then plan a flank or rear attack on them. You cannot batter down their stone-wall—you must either soar over it, tunnel under it, or else go around it.

Continuity, or Patience, when highly developed causes one to "stick to" a thing once undertaken; to manifest patience and perseverance, and to give up the mind to one thing to the exclusion of others. It is difficult to interest these people in new things—they instinctively distrust the *new* idea or thing, and cling to the old. These people are very conservative and dislike change. They can be dealt with best by avoiding shocking them with entirely *new* things, and by carefully attaching the newer idea or thing to the old so that it seems a part of the latter. New things under old names do not disturb these people as much as old things under new names—it is the form and name, rather than the substance with them. Old wine in new bottles they abhor—but new wine in old bottles they will stand. Arguments based on "old established" things, or "good old-time" things, appeal to them. Things must be "respectable," "well- established," "standing the test of years," "no new-fangled notion," etc., to appeal to them. Beware of trying new and startling changes on them—they will be prejudiced against you at once. Fall in with their ideals, and they will be excellent friends and steady customers. The words "conservative" and "established" sound well to their ears. On the contrary, people in whom this faculty is deficient will incline toward new things because they are new. This faculty, either in excess or when deficient, strongly affects the judgment, and must be taken into consideration by the Salesman.

The Religio-Moral Faculties. This group of faculties includes *Conscientiousness*, or Moral Principle; *Hope*, or Optimism;

Spirituality, or other-worldliness; *Veneration*, or Reverence; and *Benevolence*, or Human Kindness. The organs manifesting these qualities are located in the front-top of the head.

Conscientiousness, or Moral Principle, when highly developed gives one a high sense of right, justice, truth, virtue, and duty. In dealing with these people be particularly careful to make no misstatements, misrepresentations, and exaggerations, but to adhere closely to the facts of the case. Avoid also any appearance of trickiness or sharp practice, stories of shrewd bargains, etc. These people become staunch, firm friends if dealt with as they deserve, but become prejudiced against people and houses whom they suspect of unfair dealings, or in whom they lose confidence. Their keynote is "right's right"—and you should adhere to it in all dealings with them. They are "the salt of the earth," and it is a pity that there are not more of them. It is true that sometimes this faculty seems to become perverted into phariseeism and hypocrisy—but, then, every good thing has its counterfeit, and the thing to do is to distinguish between the true and the false, here as elsewhere.

Hope, or Optimism, when highly developed causes one to look on the bright side of things, expect favorable outcomes, look confidently forward, and expect much from the future. Its perversion manifests in visionary dreams and castle-building. These people are amenable to appeals to future success, bright prospects, cheerful outlook, and new undertakings which seem promising. They become enthusiastic when propositions are properly presented to them, and prefer to deal with Salesmen of similar mental characteristics. These people are natural "bulls" in business—beware of posing as a "bear" when dealing with them. They relish a good cheering, cheerful talk more than anything else. They are good people to deal with, particularly if the quality in question is balanced by caution and trained by experience.

Spirituality, or Other-worldliness, when highly developed tends to cause one to live on mental heights above the things of ordinary material existence; to trust to the "inner light;" to incline toward mysticism; and to experience a religious consciousness above the ordinary. When manifested in a lesser degree it is evidenced by the ordinary "religious" feeling. Perverted, it manifests as superstition, credulity and "psychism." The people in whom this faculty is active seem to feel that business is a degrading necessity, and they are never thoroughly at home in it, unless the goods handled happen to be along the lines of their general inclination, as for instance, religious books, etc. Consequently, their business traits and tastes arise from the other faculties, rather than from this particular one. However, they are easily prejudiced against one whom they imagine does not agree with them in their beliefs and convictions, and are apt to be swayed rather more by feeling, emotion and sentiment than by cool judgment and pure reason. They are usually strong in their likes and dislikes, and are susceptible to appeals to their imagination.

Veneration, or Reverence, when highly developed causes one to manifest reverence and extreme respect to authority of all kinds. These people are usually good church members and law abiding citizens. In business, the faculty is apt to cause them to place great stress upon authority and example. If some large merchant has ordered certain goods, they will be impressed by his example. They regard testimonials and recommendations highly. In dealing with them one must avoid speaking lightly of any thing or person esteemed by them, for they will be quick to resent it. They are usually decidedly conventional, and aim to meet the full requirements of "respectability" and social customs.

Benevolence, or Human Kindness, when highly developed causes one to manifest sympathy, kindness, generosity, and philanthropy. These people are altruistic and always ready to do another a good turn. They are moved by their feelings rather than by their reason and judgment, and will often base their business transactions rather more upon friendliness and personal feeling than upon cold business judgment and policy. They are generous where their sympathies and feelings are interested, and are too often taken advantage of by selfish people who play on their unselfish natures. Too often are they considered "easy," and are imposed on accordingly. The personal equation of the Salesman plays an important part in dealing with these people.

From these several groups of faculties arise many combinations of character in people. While it is true that there is almost infinite variety among people, nevertheless, it is true that there are a few general classes into which the majority of buyers may be fitted or grouped for convenience. Let us now consider some of the more common classes, and see how the faculties, in combination, manifest themselves.

The Argumentive Buyer. This man finds his greatest pleasure in arguing, combating and disputing with the Salesman—argument for the sake of argument, not for the sake of truth or advantage. This trait arises from developed Combativeness and Destructiveness. Do not take these people too seriously. Let them enjoy a victory over you on minor points, and then after yielding gracefully coax them along the main lines of the selling talk. At the best, they are arguing over terms, definitions, forms, etc. and not over *facts*. Let them make their own definitions, terms and forms—and then take their order for the goods which you have fitted into their side of the argument. If, however, the argument is based upon true reasoning and with a legitimate intent, then reason with him calmly and respectfully.

The Conceited Buyer. This fellow is full of Approbativeness. We have told you about him elsewhere. Meet him on his own plane, and give him the particular bait indicated for his species—he will rise to it. Appearing to defer to him, you may work in your arguments and selling talk without opposition. Prefacing your explanation with "As you know by your own experience;" or "as your own good judgment has decided;" etc., you may tell your story without much opposition. You must always let him feel that you realize that you are in the presence of a great man.

The "Stone Wall" Buyer. This man has Self Esteem and Firmness largely developed. We have told you about him under those two headings. You must fly over, tunnel under, or walk around his stone wall of reserve and stubbornness. Let him keep his wall intact—he likes it, and it would be a shame to deprive him of it. A little careful search will generally show that he has left his flanks, or his rear unguarded. He will not let you in the front door —so go around to the kitchen door, or the side-door of the sitting room—they are not so well guarded.

The Irritable Buyer. This is an unpleasant combination of Approbativeness and Combativeness, in connection with poor digestion and disordered nerves. Do not quarrel with him, and let his manner slide over you like water off a duck's back. Stick to your selling talk, and above everything keep cool, confident, and speak in even tones. This course will tend to bring him down. If you show that you are not afraid of him, and cannot be made angry—if your tones are firm yet under control and not loud—he will gradually come down to meet you. If you lose your own temper, you may as well walk out. Simply ignore his "grouch"—deny it out of existence, as our New Thought friends would say.

The "Rough Shod" Buyer. This man has large Destructiveness, and Self Esteem, and wants to run things himself. He will try to ride rough shod over you. Keep cool, even-tempered, self-possessed, and firm yet respectful. Do not let him "rattle" you. It is often more of a "bluff" than anything else. Keep on "sawing wood;" and do not be scared off. These people are often but "lath-and-plaster" instead of the iron and steel they appear to be at first sight. Keep firm and calm, is the keynote in dealing with them.

The Cautious Buyer. This man generally has Cautiousness and Continuity well developed, and Hope deficient. He is conservative and fearful. Avoid frightening him with ideas of "new" things or "experiments." If you are selling new things or ideas, manage to blend them in with things with which he is familiar—associate the new and unfamiliar with the old and familiar. And be conservative and careful in your talk, do not give him the idea that you are a radical or a "new fangled idea" man. To him, be an "old fashioned person."

The Cunning Buyer. This fellow has large Secretiveness or Cunning—he belongs to the fox tribe. He likes to scheme out things for himself, so if you will content yourself with giving him broad hints, accompanied by expressive glances, regarding what can be done with your goods, he will be apt to scheme out something in that direction, and thinking he has done it all himself, he will be pleased and interested. Let him know that you appreciate his shrewdness, particularly if he shows that his Approbativeness is well developed. But, if not, better let him think that he is deceiving you regarding his true nature. The majority of cunning people, however, take pride in it, and relish a little grim appreciation of their quality.

The Dignified Buyer. This man has large Self Esteem, and probably also large Approbativeness. In either case, let him play the part for which Nature has cast him, and you play yours. Your part is in recognizing and respecting his dignity, by your manner and tone. Whether the dignity be real or assumed, a recognition of and falling in with it is appreciated and relished. Imagine that you are in the presence of your revered great-grandfather, or the bishop, and the rest will be easy. We once knew of a jovial, but indiscreet, salesman who lost a large sale to a buyer of this kind, by poking him in the ribs and calling him "old chap." The buyer barely escaped an attack of apoplexy—the Salesman entirely escaped a sale.

The "Mean" Buyer. This man is moved by Acquisitiveness. He is suspicious of you from the start, for he feels that you intend to get some money from him. Don't blame him—he's built that way. Instead, get his mind off the subject and on to another, by plunging in at once with the statement that you have something upon which *he can make money*, or something that *will save him money*. Emphasize these points, and you will have aroused his curiosity. Then proceed along the same lines—something to make money for him, or something to save money for him—these are the only two arguments he can assimilate.

The Intelligent Buyer. These people depend almost entirely upon reason and judgment. They are scarce. When you meet one of them, drop all attempts to play upon weak points, prejudices or feelings, and confine yourself strictly to logical and rational statements, presentation of your proposition, and argument thereon. Do not attempt sophistry, argument from false premises, or other fallacies. He will detect them at once, and will feel indignant. Talk straight from the shoulder, and confine yourself to facts, figures, principles, and logic.

So far we have dealt with the voluntary or outer mind of the buyer. Let us now consider his involuntary or inner mind. There are many other terms used by psychologists to designate these two phases of mind—the important fact is that there are *two* phases or planes of mind which are operative in a sale. Let us see how they work, rather than what they are, or what they are called.

Discarding, for the time being, the current psychological theories and terminology, let us take a plain look at the facts of the case. A little consideration will show us that there are two parts to a man's mind—or two phases of activity. In the first place, there is a part of one's mind which acts as does the mind of the higher animal, the savage, the child. That is, it acts upon impulse and without restraint of the will. Its attention is easily attracted, but held with difficulty unless the interest and curiosity is awakened. It is curious, fond of novelty, inquisitive, impulsive, easily persuaded in certain directions, susceptible to impressions, amenable to suggestion, imitative, subject to panic, apt to "follow my leader," emotional, depending upon feeling rather than upon reason, subject to persuasion and coaxing, and acting almost automatically in response to awakened desire. Let us think of this part of the mind as the inheritance of the race from the past—the instinctive mind—the elemental mind of the race before Intellect mounted its throne. This part of the mind is possessed by every individual of the race. No matter how highly developed the individual may be, he has this part of the mind. No matter how much he may be in control of it, it is always there as a background and basis of his other kind of mind. The difference in the self-control of individuals depends almost altogether upon the other part of the mind, which we shall now consider—the Voluntary Mind, in which the Intellect and Will are the predominant elements. The phase which we have just considered may be called the Involuntary Mind, in which Desire and Feeling are the predominant elements.

The Voluntary Mind has come to man in the course of evolution. It is not nearly so highly developed in the majority of people, as one might at first suppose. The majority of the race have the Involuntary Mind predominant, and are swayed more by feeling and desire than by intellect and will. Those in whom the Voluntary Mind is highly developed place the intellect over the feelings—the will over the desires. They submit their feelings to the inspection and approval of their intellect, and hold their desires in check by their will. We are in the habit of thinking of will as a something which acts—but in the majority of instances it is found to be employed in checking action of the desires—in holding back rather than in pushing forward. One of the chief duties of the developed will is that of inhibition, or restraint. And inhibition depends upon the decision of the judgment or intellect. The animal, savage, or child has but little power of this kind—the average individual has more than the child or savage but less than the developed individual—the developed individual has better self-control, and subordinates his emotional desires and feelings to his judgment and will, by inhibition or restraint. Every individual has both of these phases of mind—the Involuntary and Voluntary—the latter, however, being manifested in an infinite variety of degrees of development and power. Back of every Involuntary Mind is to be found the protecting Voluntary Mind—and likewise, back of every Voluntary Mind, no matter how strong it may be, there is ever the Involuntary Mind chafing under restraint and striving to escape its master's eye and express itself in its own way. And the master often relaxes its attention, or gets tired of its strenuous task, and then the hidden nature "plays while the cat's away."

Perhaps the Salesman may be able to remember this classification of the two phases of the mind, by picturing them as *two partners* engaged in business. The Salesman is trying to secure the trade of the firm. The one brother is an easy-going fellow, possessing curiosity and childish interest, capable of being "jollied," persuaded and coaxed, and apparently acting always from his momentary desires and feelings, desirous of appearing well in the eyes of others, and anxious to make a good impression, finding it easier to say "Yes," than "No"—easier to fall in with the wishes of others than to oppose them, being vain and complaisant. This partner's name is "Easyboy." The other partner is an entirely different sort of fellow. He is cold and calculating, manifesting very little feeling or emotion, submitting everything to his reason and judgment, not moved by prejudices for or against, driving a close bargain and resenting attempts to coax or drive him. His name is "Hardfellow."

In the firm of "Easyboy and Hardfellow," the work is divided. "Easyboy" has much to do about the place, attending to many things for which his temperament specially fits him. "Hardfellow," however, does the buying, for experience has taught him that "Easyboy" is not fitted for the task, being too much under the sway of his feelings and being too easily influenced. "Easyboy" never could say "No," anyway—but "Hardfellow" finds it almost as hard to say "yes." So "Hardfellow" does the buying, but "Easyboy" always "hangs 'round" when a salesman is talking, for he is naturally inquisitive, and, being jealous, rather resents "Hardfellow's" authority in the matter. Sometimes he breaks in, and "Hardfellow" lets him have his say, and at times indulges him in minor purchases, for being a partner he must accord him some consideration in spite of the arrangement regarding duties. A strange thing is that "Easyboy" is possessed of the notion that he would make an ideal buyer, far better than "Hardfellow" in fact, and he loses no opportunity of manifesting his supposed quality, notwithstanding the fact that he usually makes a bungle of it.

For "Hardfellow" is often so busy that he cannot give his full attention to the business of buying; then again he becomes tired and at such times his judgment is not so good, and he is apt to be influenced by "Easyboy" at such times; and, again, he becomes interested in one feature of the purchase and overlooks the others—at such times "Easyboy" "gets in his fine work," and takes a hand in the buying. The Salesmen who visit the firm are fully aware of this condition of affairs, and plan things so as to have "Easyboy" on hand and able to play his part. They can do anything with him, and the more he is in evidence the better are their chances. If he had his way he would buy corner lots in the moon, or gold-bricks minus the plating. He likes to say "Yes" when coaxed, jollied or led. But the Salesmen having a straight business proposition of merit get along well with "Hardfellow," for he is reachable on such lines when logically presented and explained in a business way. Even such Salesmen, however, find "Easyboy" a valuable ally, for he often gets them a hearing when "Hardfellow" is busy or otherwise not disposed to listen. And so, they all find it an important question to get "Easyboy" on the scene at "Hardfellow's" elbow. Some claim to have discovered a method whereby they can "sidetrack" "Hardfellow" and get "Easyboy" to do the buying. And rumor even has it that there have been unscrupulous individuals who have happened around when "Hardfellow" was taking his *siesta* after a full dinner, and who then played upon "Easyboy's" weakness in a shameful manner. The firm deny these rumors, but there is an old gold brick holding back a door at the back part of the store; and a big bundle of worthless shares in a nicely printed gold- mine and a deed for a quarter-section of the blue sky, in the safe—so there may have been something in the tale, after all.

Every mind is an "Easyboy and Hardfellow" firm. Both partners are in evidence. In some cases "Easyboy" has far more sway and influence than his more capable partner; in others they have equal authority; in a third, "Hardfellow" asserts his right and ability, and "Easyboy" has to take a back seat under protest. But the same principle is true of them all. And this fact is taken into consideration by men of the world who understand the true state of affairs. If anyone doubts this statement of psychological facts, let him analyze himself, and look back over his own experience. He will find that "Easyboy" has played him many a sad trick in the past, and the "Hardfellow" has been "off his job" more than once. Then let him begin to analyze others with whom he comes in contact—he will see the same state of affairs existing there. And yet there is no mystery about the matter—it is all in accordance with known psychological laws. Some writers on the subject of Salesmanship rather solemnly assure us that the "Easyboy" part of the mind is a "higher mind"—but it is not. It belongs to the *instinctive* stage of mental development, rather than to the *rational*. It is an inheritance from the past—that past in which men were moved entirely by feeling and emotion, before reason came to its present stage of development. If it is "higher" why is it a fact that the lower races and individuals manifest it to a greater extent than the higher ones? This part of the mind gives vitality and energy to one, but unless it be controlled by Intellect and Will it is apt to prove a curse.

CHAPTER 6

THE PRE-APPROACH

Nearly all teachers of or writers upon Salesmanship lay much stress upon what is called "The Pre-Approach," by which term is indicated the preliminaries leading up to the Approach or Interview with the Buyer.

What we have said under the head of "The Mind of the Salesman" is really a part of the Pre-Approach, for it is in the nature of the preparation of the mind of the salesman for the interview with the buyer. But there is more than this to the Pre-Approach. The Pre-Approach is the mapping out of the campaign—"organizing victory" it has been called. It is the accumulation of ammunition for the fight, and the laying out of the strategy. Macbain says: "The Pre-Approach is the groundwork upon which the salesman builds. It comprises all the information obtainable by him that will be of importance in making his approach in selling the customer. * * * A sale, in fact, resembles chimney-building, in which it takes more time for preliminary scaffold- making than it does to build the permanent structure once the scaffold is made."

In the first place, an important part of the Pre-Approach is a correct and complete knowledge of your goods. Too many men rush to the Approach without knowing what they have to sell. It is not enough to know brands and prices—one should *know* his goods from top to bottom, inside and outside, from the raw material to the finished article. He should feel perfectly at home with his goods, so that he may have full information regarding them on tap, and thus have his mind free for the strategy of the sale. A little close, earnest intelligent study of one's line of goods will not only supply one with an efficient weapon, but will also impart to him a sense of certainty and confidence that he cannot have otherwise. What would be thought of a teacher of natural history who did not understand animals? And yet many salesmen are equally as ignorant about their subject.

The salesman should understand his goods so thoroughly that he could write a treatise on them, or demonstrate them before an audience of experts or of persons entirely in ignorance of them—the latter being probably the hardest task. He should be able to explain their particular virtues and characteristics to a man old in the same line, or to explain them simply and plainly to one who had never seen them or who was ignorant of their uses. We know of one salesman who was asked by his little boy to explain a cash register to him, and who complied with the request. He told us that he learned more about his cash register in the process of that explanation than he had acquired in even the process of the technical demonstration in the "salesman's school" at the factory. It is not always policy for the salesman to air his knowledge of his goods to his customer—such a course would generally bore the latter—but he should know all about his goods, nevertheless. The man who knows his goods in this way plants his feet on the solid rock and cannot be swept away, while the man who builds on the shifting sand of "half- knowledge" is always in danger.

But the more popular branch of the Pre-Approach is the knowledge of the customer. Get as many points regarding the characteristics, habits, likes and dislikes of the customer as possible. Find out as much as you can about his trade, and manner of conducting his business, as well as his business history. Macbain says: "There is really no information about a prospective customer that can be said to be valueless. On the other hand, a knowledge of one or two of the characteristics of the man to be approached may be considered sufficient, the ready intuition of the salesman being relied upon for the rest. It is assumed, of course, that a salesman will be able to call his man by name, pronouncing the name correctly upon the very first interview. This is the prime requisite, and the remaining knowledge should be grouped about this in the order of its importance."

The data regarding your prospective customer is obtainable in many ways. Much of it you may obtain from your house if they have had previous dealings with him. Other salesmen will also add to the data, but one must be on the lookout here and not allow himself to be prejudiced against the customer, or frightened by adverse reports regarding his manner and characteristics coming from other salesmen. Pierce says: "It would seem that the good characteristics of the prospect are desirable to learn. But it is a conviction that by denying to one's self the unfavorable things said about your prospect, you will not accentuate the very qualities you hope to obviate. One attempt at a sale is recalled where the prospect was said to be 'the meanest man on earth.' Almost terrified by the description, the salesman went at the prospect the wrong way; displeased him; lost the sale."

Hotel clerks—or better still, hotel proprietors—are often very well informed regarding merchants in their town, and often valuable information may be obtained in this way, although the judgment and experience of the hotel people must be appraised before basing one's own opinion regarding the customer. Other customers may also be diplomatically pressed into service in obtaining information regarding their competitors, although allowance must always be made for the personal bias in such cases. It is a good idea for the salesman to make a record of these advance reports, so as to have them on file where he may refer to them when needed. Some salesmen have a card index devoted to this purpose, which they have found very useful.

Another, and a very important point about the Pre-Approach is that of developing the proper Mental Attitude in yourself. You must get *yourself* right first, before you can get anything else right. Pierce says regarding this: "Someone has said that the greatest bane to selling goods is fear. As a matter of fact, the only thing you are afraid of is that you won't make the sale,—get the check. But, if you waive this point, and say, 'Now, I don't care whether I get this sale or not. I do know this: I am honest, my goods are honest, and if this man does not want them there are plenty of men who do,' you will find the fear melting like the mist before sunshine. Fear cannot live in the presence of your smile, your confidence, your knowledge of the business and your industry."

In this connection, re-read what we have said to you regarding the "I" and "Self-Respect" in the chapter entitled "The Mind of the Salesman." This chapter was written to cover just such cases as the one in question. If you can realize the "I" within you, your fear will disappear quickly. Remember, "there's nothing to fear but Fear."

Many successful salesmen state that they overcame their early fear and timidity by filling themselves with auto-suggestions that they were calling on the customer for the purpose of doing him a good turn—that it was a good thing for the customer that the salesman was calling on him, although he did not know it—and that he, the salesman must let nothing stand in the way of doing that good turn to the customer, etc. As ridiculous as this may appear to some, it will be found to work well in many cases. And it is based upon truth, too, for if the goods are right, and the prices are likewise, the salesman is doing the customer a good turn.

And right here, let us impress upon you the necessity of working yourself up to the point of *believing thoroughly in your own proposition*. You must get yourself into the state of mind in which, if you were in the customer's place, you would surely want to take advantage of it. You must convert yourself before you can expect to convert the customer. We know an ad. man who tells us that he never feels satisfied with an ad. that he is writing until he can make himself believe that he wants to buy the article himself. And he is right. And the salesman will do well to take a leaf from his book. Enthusiasm and belief are contagious. If you believe thoroughly in a thing, you run a much better chance of making others believe in it also, than if you feel otherwise. You must learn to *sell to yourself* first, then you may sell to the customer.

W.C. Holman, in "Salesmanship," says: "One cannot make others believe what he himself believes, unless he himself is an earnest believer. Dwight L. Moody swayed enormous audiences by the simple power of his own wonderful earnestness. No one could listen to Moody without saying: 'This man believes absolutely every word he is speaking. If he feels what he says so tremendously, there must be something in it.' If every salesman realized how largely the attitude of the 'prospect' depended upon the salesman's own mental attitude, he would be as careful to get into the right frame of mind when he started out to approach a prospect as he would be to carry a sample case. It is a simple matter for him to do this. All that is necessary is for him to 'take account of stock' just before he starts out—to enumerate to himself all the strong, convincing points in his proposition—to consider the good high qualities of the goods he is selling—run over in his mind the splendid characteristics of his house—think of the great number of customers who have bought his product—and of the supremely satisfying reasons why other customers should buy his goods. In other words, before a salesman starts to sell other men, he should sell himself. He should make this sale to himself at the beginning of every day's work."

The student should acquaint himself thoroughly with the creative force of Suggestion and Auto-Suggestion in Character Building, and in producing and maintaining the proper Mental Attitude. The volume of this series entitled "*Suggestion and Auto-Suggestion*" gives both the theory, principles and methods of applying Auto-Suggestion in the directions named. One need no longer be a slave of his Mental Attitude. On the contrary he may create and preserve the Mental Attitude he deems advisable and necessary at any time.

Mr. W.C. Holman, one of the best of the inspirational writers on Salesmanship, gives the following interesting instance of the use of Auto- Suggestion by a salesman. He says: "One of the best salesmen the writer ever knew got up what he called his catechism. He used to put himself through it every morning before starting out. Oftentimes he repeated it aloud if he had the opportunity. The questions he would repeat in a quiet tone, but the answers he would pronounce with all the earnestness of which he was capable. His catechism ran somewhat as follows:

"Am I working for a good house? YES!

"Has my house the reputation and prestige of being one of the best in its line? YES!

"Have we made hundreds of thousands of sales like the sales I am going to make to-day? YES!

"Have we an enormous body of satisfied users? YES!

"Am I selling the best goods of the kind made anywhere in the world?

YES!

"Is the price I am asking a fair one? YES!

"Do the men I am going to call on need the article I am selling? YES! "Do they realize that now? NO!

"Is that the very reason I am going to call on them—because at present they don't want my goods, and haven't yet bought them? YES!

"Am I justified in asking a prospect's time and attention to present my proposition? BY ALL THE POWERS, YES!

"Am I going to get into the office of every man that I call on, if there is any earthly way to do it? YES!

"Am I going to sell every man I call on to-day? YOU BET I AM!"

Referring to the above "catechism" of Mr. Holman, we would say that if a man would work himself up to the point of asking and answering these questions in earnest, and would carry the spirit thereof through the day, he would render himself almost invincible. A spirit like that is the spirit of the Light Brigade, of Napoleon, of the Berserker Norseman who made a way for himself. Such a man would make opportunities, instead of begging for them. Such a man would be inspired. This is Auto-Suggestion raised to the Nth Power. Try it—you need it in your business!

The second phase of the Pre-Approach is that of obtaining an interview with the prospective customer, generally known as "the prospect." In many instances the salesman is able to secure the interview by simply walking into the presence of the prospect, the latter being in full view in his store or office and no intermediary being present to intercept the approach. In such cases the second phase of the Pre-Approach is passed over, and the actual Approach is entered into at once. But in other cases, particularly in the large office buildings of the principal cities, the prospect is found to be in his private office, and the salesman's advance is halted by a clerk, or even an office boy, and there are certain preliminaries to be gone through with before an interview may be obtained. In many cases, "big" men (or those who wish to be considered "big") surround themselves with so much formality and red- tape that it is quite a feat to run the gauntlet of the guardians of the inner temple, and much tact, diplomacy, presence of mind, and often strategy is required of the Salesman in order that he may "get at his man."

Macbain, in his work entitled "Selling," says of this stage: "Between the pre-approach and the actual approach sometimes lies a trying time for the salesman. It is no uncommon thing for a prospective customer to keep a salesman waiting, either outside the office door and out of sight, or inside and in the presence of the prospective buyer. This is known as 'breaking the salesman's nerve.' It is often done with the idea of deliberately making the salesman nervous and consequently unable to make such an approach as otherwise would be possible. Perhaps one of the most common forms of this is seen when the prospective customer appears to be very busily interested in something at his desk and allows the salesman to stand an indefinite length of time and then turns suddenly upon him. This is especially disconcerting to the young man, but the experienced salesman recognizes it as an indication that either the man is very busy and actually hates to take his mind off his work, or that he is afraid of being talked into something that he will later regret. The salesman consequently shapes his introduction accordingly and will in no wise be disconcerted by this attempt as it will enable him to study carefully the outward characteristics of the man whom he is about to approach."

In many cases this waiting is forced on the salesman by a prospect who also knows something of the laws of psychology—for such knowledge is not confined to the salesman by any means, the buyer having posted himself in many cases. In the game of checkers or draughts quite an important advantage accrues to the player securing what is technically known as "the move," which, however, is a very different thing from the "first play." There is in the psychology of the sale, or of the interview between two people of equal strength, a something which corresponds very closely with "the move" in checkers. This something gives a decided advantage to the person securing it, and it is worth striving for. This something is subtle and almost indescribable, although apparent to every one who has dealings with his fellow men. It seems to be a matter of mental balance and poise. The salesman, if he be well balanced and poised, is "positive" to the buyer, the latter being in a listening, and therefore passive, attitude. So far the salesman has "the move," which however he may later lose if the prospect plays scientifically. Well, to get back to the "waiting" stage, the prospect by disturbing the salesman's poise, and "breaking his nerve" by keeping him waiting on the anxious bench in a state of suspense, often manages to get "the move" on him, unless he understands the psychology of the process and accordingly avoids it. Suspense is the most nerve-breaking mental state on the psychological list, as all realize who have experienced it. Beware of losing "the move."

An important factor in getting past the stockade of the outer office is the consciousness of Self Respect and the realization of the "I" of which we have spoken. This mental attitude impresses itself upon those who guard the outer works, and serves to clear the way. As Pierce says: "Remember, you are asking no favors; that you have nothing to apologize for, and that you have every reason in the world for holding your head high. And it is wonderful what this holding up of the head will do in the way of increasing sales. We have seen salesmen get entrance to the offices of Broadway buyers simply through the holding of the head straight up from the shoulders." But it is the Mental Attitude back of the physical expression that is the spirit of the thing —don't forget this.

The Mental Attitude and the physical expression thereof instinctively influence the conduct of other people toward one. We may see the same thing illustrated in the attitude and action of the street boy toward dogs. Let some poor cur trot along with drooping ears, timid expression, meek eyes, and tail between his legs, and the urchin will be apt to kick him or throw a rock at his retreating form. Note the difference when the self-respecting dog, with spirit in him, trots past, looking the boy fearlessly in the eye and showing his sense of self-respect and power to back it up in every movement. That dog is treated accordingly. There are certain people whose manner is such that they do not need to ask respect and consideration—it is given them as a matter of right and privilege. People stand aside to give them room, and move up in street cars that they may have a seat. And it does not necessarily follow that the person to whom this respect is shown is a worthy individual or a person of fine qualities—he may be a confidence man or a swindler. But whatever he is, or may be, he has certain outward mannerisms and characteristics which enable him to "put up a good front" and which carry him through. At the back of it all will be found certain mental states which produce the genuine outward characteristics and manner in the case of genuine instances of persons possessing authority and high position, the confidence man merely presenting a passable counterfeit, being a good actor.

It is often necessary for the salesman to send in a card to the inner office. It is well for him to have some cards, well engraved in the most approved manner, bearing simply his name: "Mr. John Jay Jones," with his business appearing thereon. If he is travelling from a large city, and is selling in smaller towns, he may have "New York," "Chicago," "Philadelphia," "Boston," etc., as the case may be in the corner of his card. If the name of his business appears on the card the prospect often goes over the matter of a possible sale, mentally, without the salesman being present to present his case, and then may decline to grant an interview. The name, without the business, often arouses interest or curiosity and thus, instead of hindering, really aids in securing the interview.

Regarding the discussion of the business with anyone other than the prospect himself, the authorities differ. As a matter of fact it would seem to depend largely upon the particular circumstances of each case, the nature of the articles to be sold, and the character and position of the subordinate in question.

One set of authorities hold that it is very poor policy to tell your business to a subordinate, and that it is far better to tell him courteously but firmly that your business is of such a nature that you can discuss it only with the prospect in person. Otherwise, it is held that the subordinate will tell you that the matter in question has already been considered by his principal, and that he is fully informed regarding the proposition, and has given orders that he is not to be disturbed further regarding it.

The other set of authorities hold that in many cases the subordinate may be pressed into service, by treating him with great respect, and an apparent belief in his judgment and authority, winning his good-will and getting him interested in your proposition, and endeavoring to have him "speak about it" to his superior during the day. It is claimed that a subsequent call, the day following, will often prove successful, as the subordinate will have paved the way for an interview and have actually done some work for you in the way of influence and selling talk. It is held that some salesmen have made permanent "friends in camp" of these subordinates who have been approached in this way.

It would seem, however, as we have said, to depend much upon the particular circumstances of the case. In some cases the subordinate is merely a "hold-off," or "breakwater;" while in others he is a confidential employee whose opinion has weight with the prospect, and whose good-will and aid are well worth securing. In any event, however, it is well to gain the respect and good-will of those in the "outer court," for they can often do much in the way of helping or injuring your chances. We have known cases in which subordinates "queered" a salesman who had offended them; and we have known other cases in which the subordinate being pleased by the salesman "put him next." It is always better to make a friend rather than an enemy—from the office-boy upward—on general principles. Many a fine warrior has been tripped up by a small pebble. Strong men have died from the bite of a mosquito.

The following advice from J.F. Gillen, the Chicago manager of the Burroughs Adding Machine Company, is very much to the point. Mr. Gillen, in the magazine "Salesmanship," says: "A salesman who has not proved his mettle—and who, unfortunately, is not sure of himself—is likely to be overcome by a sense of his own insignificance on entering the private domain of the great man, rich man, or influential man, from whom he hopes to get an order. The very hum and rush of business in this boss's office are very aweinspiring. The fact that there exists an iron-clad rule, designed to protect the boss against intrusion, forbidding the admittance of an uninvited salesman—and the fact that the army of employees are bound by this rule to oppose the entrance of any such visitor—combine to make an untried salesman morally certain of his powerlessness; to make him feel that he has no justifiable reason for presenting himself at all. Indeed he has none, if the awe which he feels for red-tape, rules, dignitaries, has made him lose sight of the attractions of his own proposition; has swallowed up his confidence in what he has to offer and his ability to enthuse the prospect in regard to it. * * * If you believe that your proposition will prove interesting to the prospect and that he will profit by doing business with you, you have a right to feel that the rule barring salesmen from his presence was not intended to bar *you.* Convince yourself of this and the stern negative of the information clerk will not abash you. You will find yourself endowed with a courage and resourcefulness to cope with a slick secretary who gives glibly evasive replies when you try to find out whether Mr. Prospect is now in his office, whether he cannot see you at once, and what reason exists for supposing you could possibly tell your business to any subordinate in place of him. Once you are thus morally sure of your ground, the hardest part of the battle is won. * * * *You can see the prospect and get speech with him, no matter what obstacles intervene, if your nerve holds out and you use your brains.*"

Remember this, always: The Psychology of Salesmanship applies not only to work with the prospect, but also to work with those who bar the way to him. Subordinates have minds, faculties, feelings and strong and weak points of mentality—they have their psychology just as their employer has his. It will pay you to make a careful study of their psychology—it has its rules, laws and principles. This is a point often overlooked by little salesmen, but fully recognized by the "big" ones. The short cut to the mind of many a prospect is directly through the mind of the man in the outer office.

CHAPTER 7

THE PSYCHOLOGY OF PURCHASE

There are several stages or phases manifested by the buyer in the mental process which results in a purchase. While it is difficult to state a hard and fast rule regarding the same, because of the variety of temperament, tendencies and mental habits possessed in several degrees by different individuals, still there are certain principles of feeling and thought manifested alike by each and every individual buyer, and a certain logical sequence is followed by all men in each and every original purchase. It follows, of course, that these principles, and this sequence, will be found to be operative in each and every original purchase, whether that purchase be the result of an advertisement, display of goods, recommendation, or the efforts of a salesman. The principle is the same in each and every case, and the sequence of the mental states is the same in each and every instance. Let us now consider these several mental states in their usual sequence.

The several mental states manifested by every buyer in an original purchase are given below in the order of sequence in which they are usually manifested:

I. Involuntary Attention.
II. First Impression.
III. Curiosity.
IV. Associated Interest.
V. Consideration.
VI. Imagination.
VII. Inclination.
VIII. Deliberation.
IX. Decision.
X. Action.

We use the term "*original* purchase" in this connection in order to distinguish the original purchase from a repeated order or subsequent purchase of the same article, in which latter instance the mental process is far more simple and which consists merely in recognizing the inclination, or habit, and ordering the goods, without repeating the original complex mental operation. Let us now proceed to a consideration of the several mental stages of the original purchase, in logical sequence:

I. *Involuntary Attention.* This mental state is the elementary phase of attention. Attention is not a faculty of the mind, but is instead the focusing of the consciousness upon one object to the temporary exclusion of all other objects. It is a turning of the mind on an object. The object of attention may be either external, such as a person or thing; or internal, such as a feeling, thought, memory, or idea. Attention may be either voluntary, that is, directed consciously by the will; or involuntary, that is, directed unconsciously and instinctively and apparently independently of the will. Voluntary attention is an acquired and developed power and is the attribute of the thinker, student and intellectual individual in all walks of life. Involuntary attention, on the contrary, is but little more than a reflex action, or a nervous response to some stimulus. As Halleck says: "Many persons scarcely get beyond the reflex stage. Any chance stimulus will take their attention away from their studies or their business." Sir William Hamilton made a still finer distinction, which is, however, generally overlooked by writers on the subject, but which is scientifically correct and which we shall follow in this book. He holds that there are three degrees or kinds of attention: (1) the reflex or involuntary, which is instinctive in nature; (2) that determined by desire or feeling, which partakes of both the involuntary and voluntary nature, and which although partly instinctive may be resisted by the will under the influence of the judgment; and (3) that determined by deliberate volition in response to reason, as in study, scientific games, rational deliberation, etc.

The first mental step of the purchase undoubtedly consists of involuntary or reflex attention, such as is aroused by a sudden sound, sight, or other sensation. The degree of this involuntary attention depends upon the intensity, suddenness, novelty, or movement of the object to which it responds. All persons respond to the stimuli arousing this form of attention, but in different degrees depending upon the preoccupation or concentration of the individual at the time. The striking or novel appearance of an advertisement; the window-display of goods; the appearance of the salesman—all these things instinctively arouse the involuntary attention, and the buyer "turns his mind on" them. But this turning the mind on belongs to Hamilton's first class—that of the instinctive response to the sight or sound, and not that aroused by desire or deliberate thought. It is the most elemental form of attention or mental effort, and to the salesman means simply: "Well, I *see* you!" Sometimes the prospect is so preoccupied or concentrated on other things that he barely "sees" the salesman until an added stimulus is given by a direct remark.

II. *First Impression.* This mental state is the hasty generalization resulting from the first impression of the object of attention—the advertisement, suggestion, display of goods, or the Salesman—depending in the last case upon the general appearance, action, manner, etc., as interpreted in the light of experience or association. In other words, the prospect forms a hasty general idea of the thing or person, either favorable or unfavorable, almost instinctively and unconsciously. The thing or person is associated or classed with others resembling it in the experience and memory of the prospect, and the result is either a good, bad or indifferent impression resulting from the suggestion of association. For this reason the ad. man and the window dresser endeavor to awaken favorable and pleasing associated memories and suggestions, and "puts his best foot foremost." The Salesman endeavors to do the same, and seeks to "put up a good front" in his Approach, in order to secure this valuable favorable first impression. People are influenced more than they will admit by these "first impressions," or suggestions, of appearance, manner, etc., and the man who understands psychology places great importance upon them. A favorable first impression smooths the way for the successful awakening of the later mental states.

An unfavorable first impression, while it may be removed and remedied later, nevertheless is a handicap which the Salesman should avoid.

(*Note*: The mental process of the purchase now passes from the stage of *involuntary attention*, to that of attention inspired by desire and feeling which partakes of *both the voluntary and involuntary elements*. The first two stages of this form of attention are known as Curiosity and Associated Interest, respectively. In some cases Curiosity precedes, in others Associated Interest takes the lead, as we shall see. In other cases the manifestation of the two is almost simultaneous.)

III. *Curiosity*. This mental state is really a form of Interest, but is more elemental than Associated Interest, being merely the interest of novelty. It is the strongest item of interest in the primitive races, in children, and in many adults of elemental development and habits of thought. Curiosity is the form of Interest which is almost instinctive, and which impels one to turn the attention to strange and novel things. All animals possess it to a marked degree, as trappers have found out to their profit. Monkeys possess it to an inordinate degree, and the less developed individuals of the human race also manifest it to a high degree. It is connected in some way with the primitive conditions of living things, and is probably a heritage from earlier and less secure conditions of living, where inquisitiveness regarding new, novel and strange sights and sounds was a virtue and the only means of acquiring experience and education. At any rate, there is certainly in human nature a decided instinctive tendency to explore the unknown and strange—the attraction of the mysterious; the lure of the secret things; the tantalizing call of the puzzle; the fascination of the riddle.

The Salesman who can introduce something in his opening talk that will arouse Curiosity in the prospect has done much to arouse his attention and interest. The street-corner fakir, and the "barker" for the amusement-park show, understand this principle in human nature, and appeal largely to it. They will blindfold a boy or girl, or will make strange motions or sounds, in order to arouse the curiosity of the crowd and to cause them to gather around—all this before the actual appeal to interest is made. In some buyers Curiosity precedes Associated Interest—the interest in the unknown and novel precedes the practical interest. In others the Associated Interest—the practical interest inspired by experience and association—precedes Curiosity, the latter manifesting simply as inquisitiveness regarding the details of the object which has aroused Associated Interest. In other cases, Curiosity and Associated Interest are so blended and shaded into each other that they act almost as one and simultaneously. On the whole, though, Curiosity is more elemental and crude than Associated Interest, and may readily be distinguished in the majority of cases.

IV. *Associated Interest.* This mental state is a higher form of interest than Curiosity. It is a practical interest in things relating to one's interests in life, his weal or woe, loves or hates, instead of being the mere interest in novelty of Curiosity. It is an acquired trait, while Curiosity is practically an instinctive trait. Acquired Interest develops with character, occupation, and education, while Curiosity manifests strongly in the very beginnings of character, and before education. Acquired Interest is manifested more strongly in the man of affairs, education and experience, while Curiosity has its fullest flower in the monkey, savage, young child and uncultured adult. Recognizing the relation between the two, it may be said that Curiosity is the root, and Associated Interest the flower.

Associated Interest depends largely upon the principle of Association or Apperception, the latter being defined as "that mental process by which the perceptions or ideas are brought into relation to our previous ideas and feelings, and thus are given a new clearness, meaning and application." Apperception is the mental process by which objects and ideas presented to us are perceived and thought of by us in the light of our past experience, temperament, tastes, likes and dislikes, occupation, interest, prejudices, etc., instead of as they actually are. We see everything through the colored glasses of our own personality and character. Halleck says of Apperception: "A woman may apperceive a passing bird as an ornament to her bonnet; a fruit grower, as an insect killer; a poet, as a songster; an artist, as a fine bit of coloring and form. The housewife may apperceive old rags as something to be thrown away; a ragpicker, as something to be gathered up. A carpenter, a botanist, an ornithologist, a hunter, and a geologist walking through a forest would not see the same things." The familiar tale of the text-books illustrates this principle. It relates that a boy climbed up a tree in a forest and watched the passers-by, and listened to their conversation. The first man said: "What a fine stick of timber that tree would make." The boy answered: "Good morning, Mr. Carpenter." The second man said: "That is fine bark." The boy answered: "Good morning, Mr. Tanner." The third man said: "I'll bet there's squirrels in that tree." The boy answered: "Good morning, Mr. Hunter." Each and every one of the men saw the tree in the light of his personal Apperception or Associated Interest.

Psychologists designate by the term "the apperceptive mass" the accumulated previous experiences, prejudices, temperament, inclination and desires which serve to modify the new perception or idea. The "apperceptive mass" is really the "character" or "human nature" of the individual. It necessarily differs in each individual, by reason of the great variety of experiences, temperament, education, etc., among individuals. Upon a man's "apperceptive mass," or character, depends the nature and degree of his interest, and the objects which serve to inspire and excite it.

It follows then that in order to arouse, induce and hold this Associated Interest of the prospect, the Salesman must present things, ideas or suggestions which will appeal directly to the imagination and feelings of the man before him, and which are associated with his desires, thoughts and habits. If we may be pardoned for the circular definition we would say that one's Associated Interest is aroused only by interesting things; and that the interesting things are those things which concern his interests. A man's interests always interest him—and his interests are usually those things which concern his advantage, success, personal well-being—in short his pocketbook, social position, hobbies, tastes, and satisfaction of his desires. Therefore the Salesman who can throw the mental spot-light on these interesting things, may secure and hold one's Associated Interest.

Hence the psychology of the repeated statement: "I can save you money;" "I can increase your sales;" "I can reduce your expenses;" "I have something very choice;" or "I can give you a special advantage," etc.

It may as well be conceded that business interest is selfish interest, and not altruistic. In order to interest a man in a business proposition he must be shown how it will benefit him in some way. He is not running a philanthropic institution, or a Salesman's Relief Fund, nor is he in business for his health—he is there to make money, and in order to interest him you must show him something to his advantage. And the first appeal of Associated Interest is to his feeling of Self Interest. It must be in the nature of the mention of "rats!" to a terrier, or "candy!" to a child. It must awaken pleasant associations in his mind, and pleasing images in his memory. If this effect is produced, he can be speedily moved to the succeeding phases of Imagination and Inclination. As Halleck says: "All feeling tends to excite desire. * * * A representative image of the thing desired is the necessary antecedent to desire. If the child had never seen or heard of *peaches* he would have no desire for them." And, following this same figure, we may say that if the child has a taste for peaches he will be *interested* in the idea of peaches. And so when you say "peaches!" to him you have his Associated Interest, which will result in a mental image of the fruit followed by a *desire* to possess it, and he will listen to your talk regarding the subject of "peaches."

The following are the general psychological rules regarding Associated Interests:

I. Associated Interest attaches only to interesting things—that is to things associated with one's general desires and ideas.

II. Associated Interest will decline in force and effect unless some new attributes or features are presented—it requires variety in presentation of its object.

Macbain says: "One of the old time salesmen who used to sell the trade in the Middle West, beginning some thirty years ago, and following that vocation for several decades, used as his motto, 'I am here to do you good.' He did not make his statement general, either, in telling his customers how he could do it. He got right down to the vital affairs which touched his customers. He demonstrated it to them, and this personal demonstration is the kind that makes the sales."

Remember, always, that the phase of Associated Interest in a purchase is not the same as the phase of Demonstration and Proof. It is the "warming up" process, preceding the actual selling talk. It is the stage of "thawing out" the prospect and melting the icy covering of prejudice, caution and reluctance which encases him. Warm up your prospect by *general statements* of Associated Interest, and blow the coals by positive, brief, pointed confident statements of the good things you have in store for him. And, finally, remember that the sole purpose of your efforts at this state is to arouse in him the mental state of INTERESTED EXPECTANT ATTENTION! Keep blowing away at this spark until you obtain the blaze of Imagination and the heat of Desire.

V. *Consideration.* This mental state is defined as: "An examination, inquiry, or investigation into anything." It is the stage following Curiosity and Associated Interest, and tends toward an inquiry into the thing which has excited these feelings. Consideration, of course, must be preceded and accompanied by Interest. It calls for the phase of Attention excited by feeling, but a degree of voluntary attention is also manifested therewith. It is the "I think I will look into this matter" stage of the mental process of purchase. It is usually evidenced by a disposition to ask questions regarding the proposition, and to "see what there is to it, anyway." In Salesmanship, this stage of Consideration marks the passing from the stage of Approach on the Salesman's part, to that of the Demonstration. It marks the passage from Passive Interest to Active Interest—from the stage of being "merely interested" in a thing, to that of "interested investigation." Here is where the real selling work of the salesman begins. Here is where he begins to describe his proposition in detail, laying stress upon its desirable points. In the case of an advertisement, or a window display, the mental operation goes on in the buyer's mind in the same way, but without the assistance of the salesman. The "selling talk" of the advertisement must be stated or suggested by its text. If the

Consideration is favorable and reveals sufficiently strong attractive qualities in the proposition or article, the mind of the buyer passes on to the next stage of the process which is known as:

VI. *Imagination.* This mental state is defined as: "The exercise of that power or faculty of the mind by which it conceives and forms ideal pictures of things communicated to it by the organs of sense." In the mental process of a purchase, the faculty of imagination takes up the idea of the object in which the Associated Interest has been aroused, and which has been made the subject of Consideration, and endeavors to picture the object in use and being employed in different ways, or as in possession of the buyer. One must use his imagination in order to realize what good a thing will be to him; how he may use it; how it will look; how it will sell; how it will serve its purpose; how it will "work out" or "make good" when purchased. A woman gazing at a hat will use her imagination to picture how she will look in it. The man looking at the book will use his imagination in picturing its uses and the pleasure to be derived therefrom. The business man will use his imagination to picture the probable sale of the goods, their display, their adaptability to his trade, etc. Another will picture himself enjoying the gains from his purchase. Imagination plays an important part in the psychology of the sale. It is the direct inciter of desire and inclination. The successful salesman realizes this, and feeds the flame of the imagination with the oil of Suggestion. In fact, Suggestion receives its power through the Imagination. The Imagination is the channel through which Suggestion reaches the mind. Salesmen and ad. writers strive to arouse the imagination of their prospective customers by clever word-painting. The Imagination is the "direct wire" to Desire. From Imagination it is a short step to the next mental stage which is called:

VII. *Inclination.* This mental state is defined as: "A leaning or bent of the mind or will; desire; propensity." It is the "want to" feeling. It is the mental state of which Desire is an advanced stage. Inclination has many degrees. From a faint inclination or bent in a certain direction, it rises in the scale until it becomes an imperious demand, brooking no obstacle or hindrance. Many terms are employed to designate the various stages of Inclination, as for instance: Desire, wish, want, need, inclination, leaning, bent, predilection, propensity, penchant, liking, love, fondness, relish, longing, hankering, aspiration, ambition, appetite, hunger, passion, craving, lust, etc.

Desire is a strange mental quality, and one very difficult to define strictly. It is linked with feeling on one side, and with will on the other. Feeling rises to desire, and desire rises to the phase of will and endeavors to express itself in action. Halleck says of Desire: "*It has for its object something which will bring pleasure or get rid of pain, immediate or remote, for the individual or for some one in whom he is interested. Aversion, or a striving to get away from something, is merely the negative aspect of desire.*" Inclination in its various stages is aroused through the appeals to the feelings through the imagination. The feelings related to the several faculties are excited into action by a direct appeal to them through the imagination, and inclination or desired results. Appeal to Acquisitiveness will result in a feeling which will rise to inclination and desire for gain. Appeal to Approbativeness will act likewise in its own field. And so on through the list, each well-developed faculty being excited to feeling by the appropriate appeal through the imagination, and thus giving rise to Inclination which in turn strives to express itself in action through the will.

In short, every man is a bundle of general desires, the nature and extent of which are indicated by his several faculties, and which result from heredity, environment, training, experience, etc. These desires may be excited toward a definite object by the proper emotional appeal through the imagination, and by suggestion. Desire *must* be created or aroused before action can be had, or the will manifest in action. For, at the last, we do things only because we "want to," directly or indirectly. Therefore, the important aim of the Salesman is to make his prospect "want to." And in order to make him "want to" he must make him see that his proposition is calculated to "bring pleasure, or get rid of pain, immediate or remote, for the individual or for someone else in whom he is interested." In business, the words "profit and loss" may be substituted for "pleasure and pain," although really, they are but forms of the latter. But even when the prospect is brought to the stage of strong inclination or desire, he does not always move to gratify the same. Why is this? What other mental process interferes? Let us see as we pass on to the next stage of the purchase, known as:

VIII. *Deliberation.* This mental state is defined as: "The act of deliberating and weighing facts and arguments in the mind, calmly and carefully." Here is manifested the action of thought and reason—the mental process of weighing and balancing facts, feelings, and inclinations. For it is not only *facts* and *proofs* which are weighed in the mental balance, but also feelings, desires, and fears. Pure logical reasoning inclines to strict logical processes based upon irrefragible facts, it is true—but there is but little pure logical reasoning. The majority of people are governed more by their feelings and inclinations—their loves and their fears—than by logic. It has been said: "People seek not *reasons*, but *excuses for following their feelings*." The real deliberation, in the majority of cases, is the weighing of probable advantages and disadvantages—of various likes and dislikes—of hopes and fears.

It is said that our minds are controlled by *motives*—and the strongest motive wins. We often find that when we think we desire a thing ardently, we then find that we also like something else better, or perhaps fear something else more than we desire the first thing. In such case, the strongest or most pressing feeling wins the day. The faculties here exert their different influences. Caution opposes Acquisitiveness. Acquisitiveness opposes Conscientiousness. Fear opposes Firmness. And so on. The deliberation is not only the weighing of facts, but also the weighing of feelings.

The process of Deliberation—the weighing of desires—the play and counterplay of motives—is well illustrated by a scene in a classical French comedy. "Jeppe," one of the characters, has been given money by his wife to buy her a cake of soap. He prefers to buy a drink with the coin, for his inclinations tend in that direction. But he knows that his wife will beat him if he so squanders the money. He deliberates over the pleasure to be derived from the drink, and the pain which would arise from the beating. "My stomach says drink—my back says soap," says Jeppe. He deliberates further. Then: "My stomach says Yes! My back says No!" cries the poor wight. The conflict between back and stomach rages still more fiercely. Then comes the deciding point: "Is not my stomach more to me than my back? Sure, it is! I say *Yes*!" cries Jeppe. And away to the tavern he marches. It has been remarked that if the active suggestion of the distant sight of his wife armed with the cudgel, had been added to the situation, Jeppe would have bought the soap. Or, if the tavern had not been so handy, the result might have been different. Sometimes a mental straw tips the scale. The above illustration contains the entire philosophy of the action of the mind in the process of Deliberation. The salesman will do well to remember it.

Halleck thus well states the immediate and remote factors in choice: "The immediate factors are * * * (1) a preceding process of desire; (2) the presence in consciousness of more than one represented object or end, to offer an alternative course of action; (3) deliberation concerning the respective merits of these objects; (4) the voluntary fiat of decision, which seems to embody most the very essence of will. The remote factors are extremely difficult to select. The sum total of the man is felt more in choice than anywhere else. * * * Before a second person could approximate the outcome, he would have to know certain remote factors, the principal being: (1) heredity; (2) environment; (3) education; (4) individual peculiarities." This eminent authority might well have added an additional element—a most important one—as follows: (5) SUGGESTION.

The Salesman watching carefully the shifting scale of Deliberation, injects a telling argument or suggestion into the scale, which gives weight to his side at a critical stage. He does this in many ways. He may neutralize an objection by a counter-fact. He adds another proof or fact here—a little more desire and feeling there, until he brings down the scale to a decision. It must be remembered that this Deliberation is *not regarding* the desirability of the proposition—the prospect has admitted his desire, either directly or indirectly, and is now engaged in trying to justify his desire by reason and expediency. He is seeking for reasons or "excuses" to back up his desire, or perhaps, is endeavoring to strike a balance of his conflicting desires and feelings. His mental debate is not over the question of desiring the goods, but over the expediency and probable result of buying them. It is the "to buy or not to buy" stage. This is a delicate part of the process of the purchase, and many prospects act like "see-saws" during the process. The clever Salesman must be ready with the right argument at the right place. To him this is the Argumentive Stage. Finally, if the Salesman's efforts are successful, the balance drops, and the process passes to the next stage, known as—

IX. *Decision.* This mental stage is defined as: "The mental act of deciding, determining, or settling any point, question, difference, or contest." It is the act of the *will*, settling the dispute between the warring faculties, feelings, ideas, desires and fears. It is will acting upon reason, or (alas! too often, upon mere feeling). Without entering into a metaphysical discussion, let us remind you that the practical psychology of the day holds that "the strongest motive *at the moment* wins the choice." This strongest motive may be of reason or of feeling; conscious or unconscious; but *strongest* at that moment it must be, or it would not win. And this strongest motive is strongest merely because of our character or "nature" as manifested at that particular moment, in that particular environment, under the particular circumstances, and subject to the particular suggestions. The choice depends more upon association than we generally realize, and association is awakened by suggestion. As Halleck says: "It is not the business of the psychologist to state what power the association of ideas ought to have. It is for him to ascertain what power it does have." And as Ziehen says: "We cannot think as we will, but we must think just as those associations which happen to be present prescribe." This being the case, the Salesman must realize that the Decision is based always upon (1) the mental states of the man at that moment; plus (2) the added motives supplied by the Salesman. It is "up to" the Salesman to supply those motives, whether they be facts, proofs, appeals to reason, or excitement of feeling. Hope, fear, like, dislike—these are the potent motives in most cases. In business, these things are known as "profit or loss." All the faculties of the mind supply motives which aroused may be thrown into the balance affecting decision. This is what argument, demonstration and appeal seek to do—supply motives.

(*Note*:—It might naturally be supposed that when the final stage of Decision has been reached, the mental process of purchase is at an end. But, not so. Will has three phases: Desire, Decision, and Action. We have passed through the first two, but Action still is unperformed. A familiar example is that of the man in bed in the morning. He ponders over the question of rising, and finally decides to get up. But action does not necessarily result. The trigger of Action has not been pulled, and the spring released. So thus we have another mental state, known as:—)

X. *Action.* This mental state is defined as: "Volition carried into effect." Mill says: "Now what is an action? Not one, but a series of two things: the state of mind called a volition, followed by an effect. The volition or intention to produce the effect is one thing; the effect produced in consequence of the intention is another thing; the two together constitute the action." Halleck says: "For a completed act of will, there must be action along the line of the decision. Many a decision has not aroused the motor centers to action, nor quickened the attention, for any length of time. There are persons who can frame a dozen decisions in the course of a morning, and never carry out one of them. Sitting in a comfortable chair, it may take one but a very short time to form a decision that will require months of hard work. * * * Some persons can never seem to understand that resolving to do a thing is not the same as doing it. * * * There may be desire, deliberation, and decision; but if these do not result in action along the indicated line, the process of will is practically incomplete." Many a person decides to do a thing but lacks the something necessary to release the motive impulses. They tend to procrastinate, and delay the final act. These people are sources of great care and work to the Salesman. Some men can get their prospects to the deciding point, but fail to get them to act. Others seem specially adapted to "closing" these cases. It requires a peculiar knack to "close"—the effort is entirely psychological. We shall consider it in a subsequent chapter under the head of "Closing." To be a good "closer" is the ambition of every Salesman, for it is the best paid branch of his profession.

It depends largely upon the scientific application of suggestion. To lead a prospect to Action, is to pull the trigger of his will. To this end all the previous work has been directed. Its psychology is subtle. What makes you finally get out of bed in the morning, after having "decided to" several times without resulting action? To understand this, is to understand the process of the final Action in the mind of the buyer. Is it not worth learning?

In the succeeding chapters we shall consider the several stages of the "Salesman's Progress" toward a sale—the Approach, the Demonstration, and the Closing. In these stages of the Salesman, we shall see the action and reaction upon the Mind of the Buyer, along the lines of the Psychology of the Purchase. In the Sale-Purchase the minds of the Salesman and the Buyer meet. The result is the Signed Order. The psychological process of the Sale is akin to the progress of a game of chess or checkers. And neither is the result of chance—well defined principles underlie each, and established methods are laid down for the student.

CHAPTER 8

THE APPROACH

Old salesmen hold that in the psychology of the sale there is no more important stage or phase than the introductory stage—the stage of the Approach. Pierce says: "Experienced salesmen will tell you that the first five minutes in front of a prospect is worth more than all the remainder in the matter of getting the check. Why? Because it is then that the prospect is forming his impressions of you. Usually he is obliged to form this quick size- up of the man he meets, in order to conserve his time for important duties. Therefore it is your duty to have this first impression the best within your power. And the best way to develop this is to be genuine." But it must never be lost sight of that the First Impression is solely for the purpose of obtaining an entrance for the fine edge of your wedge of salesmanship, which you must then proceed to drive home to its logical conclusion,—the Order. An impression for impression's sake is a fallacy. Remember the old story of the Salesman who wrote in that he was not making sales, but that he was "making a good impression on my customers." The firm wired back to him: "Go out and make some more impressions—on a snow bank." Do not lose sight of the real object of your work, in obtaining the preliminary results.

The National Cash Register Company instructs its salesmen regarding the First Impression, as follows: "Remember, the first five minutes of speaking to a man is likely to make or break you as far as that sale is concerned. If you are in any way antagonistic or offensive to him, you have hurt your chances badly from the start. If you have failed to definitely please or attract him, you have not done enough. It isn't sufficient to be merely a negative quantity. You should make a positive favorable impression, and not by cajolery nor attempted wit nor cleverness. The only right way to gain a man's liking is to deserve it. The majority of men do not often know just what the characteristics of a man are which makes him pleasing or displeasing to them; but they *feel* pleased or displeased, attracted or repulsed, or indifferent, and the feeling is definite and pronounced, even though they cannot understand just what makes it. A storekeeper in the smallest way of business in a little country village is just as susceptible of being pleased or offended as any merchant prince. It should never be forgotten that whatever his position may be, 'a man's a man for a' that.'"

It is not so much what a man *says* when he approaches the prospect, as the way he acts. It is his manner, rather than his speech. And back of his manner is his Mental Attitude. Without going into subtle psychological theorizing, we may say that it may be accepted as a working hypotheses that a man radiates his Mental State, and that those he approaches feel these radiations. It may be the suggestion of manner, or it may be something more subtle—no use discussing theories here, we haven't the time—the fact is that it acts as radiations would act. This being recognized it will be seen that the man's Mental Attitude in the Approach must be right. In the previous chapters we have had much to say to you regarding the factors which go to create the Mental Attitude. Now is the time to manifest what you have learned and practice—for you are making the Approach.

Carry in mind Holman's catechism, of which we have told you. Maintain your Self-Respect, and remember that you are a MAN. Pierce says of this: "One reason for this is that self-respect is necessary in your work. And self- respect cannot obtain where there is lack of confidence either in your own ability or in your line of goods. Assuming that you take only such a line as you yourself can enthusiastically endorse, it must be remembered that your goods place you absolutely on a par with the merchant. Hence, you talk to him shoulder to shoulder, as it were. You are not as a slave to a master! as a hireling to a lord; as a worm to a mountain; although this is the usual attitude untrained salesmen consciously or unconsciously assume. They are timid. They feel they might know their goods better. They feel, perhaps, that the prospect knows their goods or their competitors' goods better than they do themselves. Fear is written all over their faces as the approach is made. Nine- tenths of the fear is due to ignorance of the goods. The other tenth is lack of experience."

Regarding this matter of Fear, we would say that the experience of the majority of men who have lived active and strenuous lives, meeting with all sorts of people under all sorts of circumstances, is that the cause of Fear of people and things exists chiefly in the imagination. It is the fear of anticipation rather than the fear of actual conditions. It is like the fear felt upon approaching a dentist's office—worse than the actual experience of the chair. Suspense and fearful expectation are two of the great sources of human weakness. Experience shows us that the majority of things we fear never happen; that those which do happen are never so bad as we had feared. Moreover, experience teaches us that when a real difficulty confronts us, we usually are given the strength and courage to meet and bear it, or to overcome it—while in our moments of fearful anticipation these helpful factors are not apparent. Sufficient for the moment are the evils thereof—it is not the troubles of the moment which bear us down, but the burdens of future moments which we have added to our load. The rule is to meet each question or obstacle as it arises, and not to add fear of trouble beyond to the work of the moment. Do not cross your bridge till you come to it. The majority of feared things melt away when you come up to them—they partake of the nature of the mirage. It is the ghosts of things which never materialize which cause us the greatest fear. Banish Fearthought from your Mental Attitude when you make the Approach.

But, a word of warning here: Do not become "fresh" or impudent because you feel Self Reliant and Fearless. While realizing that *you* are a Man, do not forget that the prospect is also one. Impudence is a mark of weakness rather than of strength—strong men are above this petty thing. Be polite and courteous. The true gentleman is both self-respecting and polite. And, after all is said and done, the best Approach that a Salesman can make is that of a GENTLEMAN. This will win in the long run, and the consciousness of having so acted will tend to strengthen the Salesman and preserve his self- respect. Remember not only to manifest the self-respect of a gentleman—but also to observe the obligations of politeness and courtesy which are incumbent upon a gentleman. *Noblesse oblige*—"nobility imposes obligations."

If you want a maxim of action and manner, take this one: "Act as a gentleman should." If you want a touchstone upon which to test manner and action, take this: "Is this the act of a gentleman?" If you will follow this advice you will acquire a manner which will be far superior to one based upon artificial rules or principles—a natural manner—because the manner of a gentleman is the expression of true and pure courtesy, and will be respected as such by all, whether they, themselves, observe it or not. We have seen many instances in which the maintenance of the true gentlemanly spirit under strong provocation has completely disarmed boorishness, and won friendship and regard from those apparently opposing it at the time.

The first psychological element of a Sale is that of the First Impression upon the buyer. And the impression must be of a favorable kind. There must be nothing to create a bad impression for this will distract the attention from the purpose of the Approach to the particular object awakening the unpleasant impression. The first point preliminary to gaining attention, is to know the name of the man you are approaching; and if possible just where he is. Nothing is more demoralizing to the Salesman, and more likely to break up the psychological influence of the Approach, than a lack of knowledge of the name and identity of the man you wish to see. The miscarriage of an Approach occasioned by mistaking the person should be avoided. If you do not know your man, or where he is in the office, it will be well to inquire of the others present, politely of course, where "Mr. X's" desk is. If you happen to ask this question of "Mr. X" himself, you can easily adjust yourself to the occasion. The *fiasco* of approaching "Mr. A" and greeting him as "Mr. X" is apt to be confusing and weakening, and tends to bring the element of ridicule into the interview, unless the Salesman has the tact and wit to pass it off. If possible, avoid asking for "the proprietor," or inquiring of a man, "are you the proprietor?" If you do not know the proprietor's name, ask it of some one.

The National Cash Register people say to their salesmen: "It is manifestly improper to describe a definite form of words and require salesmen to use them in all cases when they approach business men at the first interview. What would be proper to say to one man under given circumstances might be unsuitable to say to another under different circumstances. Much must be left to the discretion of the salesman. At the same time there are certain leading statements to be made, and certain ways of making them which experience has shown to be well adapted to the end in view. * * * It is not necessary that this introductory talk should be long. Often a short talk is more convincing. We do not advise salesmen to introduce themselves by sending in a card, but prefer that they should depend wholly on what they are able to say to secure a hearing. We strongly disapprove of obscure introductions and all tricks, and believe that a man who has something worth saying, and is not ashamed of his business, can make known his errand in a bold, straightforward manner. A salesman should adapt himself to his man, but at the same time he should have a fixed idea of what he has to say. He should be dignified and earnest. * * * As soon as you do succeed in reaching the proprietor, and have said to him, 'Good morning! Is this Mr. Johnson?' then say directly and plainly, 'I represent the National Cash Register Company.' This immediately puts you on a square footing, and if he has anything to say against your business it will draw his fire immediately. If he has nothing to say, proceed to business at once, but don't under any circumstances say, 'I called to sell you a register,' or 'I called to tell you about our registers,' but put it rather in this way, '*I want to interest you in our methods for taking care of transactions with customers in your store*.' The difference between the two ways of saying it is that one begins with *your end* of the business—the thing that interests *you*; while the other begins at *his* end of it—the thing presumably interesting to him."

We specially direct the student's attention to the above paragraph. It contains in a nutshell the whole philosophy of the introductory talk of the Approach. It is the essence of the experience and knowledge of the thousands of salesmen of the great selling organization of the large concern named, and is right to the point, and what is still more important, it is scientifically correct, and based upon true psychological principles.

The Salesman in making the Approach should not act as if he were in a hurry, nor should he dawdle. He should go about it in a business-like manner showing his realization of the value of time, and yet acting as if he had the time necessary for the transaction of that particular piece of business, just as he would if the buyer had called on him instead of vice versa. Don't swagger or strut, or act as if you were the proprietor. Act the part of the real business man who is at ease and yet is attending to business. Do not try to "rush" the customer in the Approach—you are calling on him and must appear to defer to him in the matter of opening the conversation, in a respectful and yet self- respecting manner. The better poised and balanced you are in manner, the more he will respect you, no matter how he may act. It is much easier for a buyer to turn down an ill-bred boorish caller than one who shows the signs of being a gentleman. In fact the boorish caller invites the turn-down—he suggests it by his manner; while the gentleman suggests respectful treatment. The line of least resistance in suggestion is the one most natural for people to follow.

Some salesmen try to grasp the hand of the customer at the beginning. This is all right if the customer be a jovial "hale fellow, well met" kind of a man, but if he be reserved and dignified he will be apt to resent your pushing this attention upon him. The thing to do is to make him feel like shaking hands—this is an important point, which counts if gained. You can generally tell from his manner and expression whether to extend your hand. You must trust to your intuitions in "sizing up" your man. What has been said regarding the mind of the buyer will help you, and what data you have collected will also be of use, but at the last you must depend upon your own intuition to a considerable extent. Experience develops this intuitive faculty. Some salesmen thrust their cards into the hands of a prospect when they introduce themselves. This is poor psychology, for it serves to attract the prospect's attention to the card and away from the salesman. Introduce yourself verbally, simply and distinctly, and then get down to business.

If you see a man is busy with someone else, or with something in particular—wait for him. Don't break into his occupation, until he looks up and gives you the psychological signal to proceed. Never interrupt another salesman who may be talking to the prospect. This is not only a point in fair play and business courtesy, but is very good business policy in addition. When you begin your introductory talk, get right to the point, and don't beat around the bush as so many do. Get down to business—get over the agony of suspense—take the plunge. Remember always, that to the prospect your little story is not as stale or stereotyped as it may be to you—so put earnestness into it, and tell it just as if you were relating it for the first time to someone who had requested it from you. Maintain *your* interest, if you would arouse that of the prospect.

Never commit the folly of asking a prospect: "Are you busy?" or, "I fear you are busy, sir?" This is a very bad suggestion for the prospect, and makes it easy for him to say "Yes!" You mould bullets for him to fire at you. If he really *is* too busy to give you the proper attention, you may do well to tell him so, and then get out—but never suggest anything of this kind to him if you expect to proceed. It is akin to the doleful "You don't want to buy any matches, sir, do you?" of the forlorn vendors of small articles who float into offices at times. Never make it easy for a prospect to turn you down—or out. If he is going to do these things, make him work hard to do it. This might seem like needless advice, but many young salesmen commit this particular fault. Avoid the apologetic attitude and manner—you have nothing to apologize for. You are using up *your* time as much as the prospect's time—let it go at that. Never apologize for anything but a fault or mistake. Your call is not a fault or a mistake—unless you make it so by assuming it to be such. Some men would like to apologize for being alive, but they never make salesmen. Be careful what adverse suggestions you may put into the prospect's mind by this apologizing and "explaining" business. What's the use of this nonsense anyway—it never sold any goods, and never will. It is merely a sign of weakness and lack of nerve. Better stop it.

The trouble with these apologetic and explanatory fellows is that they do not thoroughly believe in the merit of their propositions. If they really believed as they should—if they had "sold themselves"—they would realize that the prospect needs their goods, and, that although he might not know it now, he is being done a favor by having his attention called to them. A Salesman has no need to apologize to a customer, unless he has need to apologize to himself—and if he is not right on the latter score he had better change his line and get something to sell that he is not ashamed of, or get out of the business altogether. No man ever feels ashamed of anything in which he thoroughly believes and appreciates.

The following advice from the National Cash Register people, is like everything else they say, very good: "Do not attempt to talk to a man who is not listening, who is writing a letter or occupying himself in any other way while you are talking. That's useless, and is a loss of self-respect and of his respect. If he cannot give you his attention, say to him: 'I see that you are busy. If you can give me your attention for a few minutes I shall be pleased; but I don't want to interrupt you, if you cannot spare the time, and I will call again.' Try to understand and feel thoroughly the distinction between confidence and familiarity. Never fail in respect either to yourself or to the man with whom you are talking. Never be familiar with him. Never put your hand on his shoulder or on his arm, nor take hold of his coat. Such things are repugnant to a gentleman—and you should assume that he is one. Never pound the desk or shake your finger at a prospect. Don't shout at him as if sound would take the place of sense. Don't advance at him and talk so excitedly under his nose that he will back away from you for fear of being run over, as if you were a trolley-car. I have seen a sales agent back a prospect half way across a room in this way. Don't compel a man to listen to you by loud or fast talking. Don't make him feel that he can't get a word in edgewise and has to listen until you are out of breath. This is not the sort of compulsion to make customers. But make him believe that you have something to say and will say it quickly. Put yourself in his place from the very start. Make him feel, not that you are trying to force *your* business upon him, but that you want to discuss how *his* business may be benefited by you."

One of the best salesmen this particular company ever had has passed down to the selling corps of that concern the following axiom: "If you do but one thing, in approaching a prospect, say, '*It will save you money*,' seven times, and you have made a good Approach." And so say we. Concrete facts, stated in terse terms, are the essence of the opening talk and the life of the Approach.

What we have said so far has reference to the stage of First Impression, which followed the preliminary stage of Involuntary Attention which was caused by your presence. The purpose of the favorable First Impression is to make the way easy for the real process of selling which is to follow. The principle of First Impression rests upon the associated experience of the buyer, and its effect arises from suggestion. The hasty, general idea or impression of the Salesman's personality, which we call the First Impression, is almost unconscious on the part of the prospect, and is due largely to the suggestion of association. That is, the prospect has met other people manifesting certain characteristics, and has fallen into the habit of hasty generalization, or classification of people in accordance with certain traits of appearance, manner, etc. This is the operation of the psychological principle of the Association of Ideas, and may be influenced by what is known as the Suggestion of Association. The following quotation from the volume of this series entitled "Suggestion and Auto-Suggestion," will make clearer this principle:

"This form of Suggestion is one of the most common phases. It is found on all sides, and at all times. The mental law of association makes it very easy for us to associate certain things with certain other things, and we will find that when one of the things is recalled it will bring with it its associated impression. * * * We are apt to associate a well-dressed man, of commanding carriage, travelling in an expensive automobile, with the idea of wealth and influence. And, accordingly, when some adventurer of the 'J. Rufus Wallingford' type travels our way, clad in sumptuous apparel, with the air of an Astorbilt, and a $10,000 (hired) automobile, we hasten to place our money and valuables in his keeping, and esteem ourselves honored by having been accorded the privilege."

The Suggestion of Authority also plays its part in the First Impression, and in all the stages of sale in fact. This form of suggestion is described in the book just mentioned, as follows: "Let some person posing as an authority, or occupying a position of command, calmly state a fallacy with an air of wisdom and conviction, without any 'ifs' or 'buts,' and many otherwise careful people will accept the suggestion without question; and, unless they are afterward forced to analyze it by the light of reason they will let this seed find lodgement in their minds, to blossom and bear fruit thereafter. The explanation is that in such cases the person suspends the critical attention which is usually interposed by the attentive will, and allows the idea to enter his mental castle unchallenged, and to influence other ideas in the future. It is like a man assuming a lordly air and marching past the watchman at the gate of the mental fortress, where the ordinary visitor is challenged and severely scrutinized; his credentials examined; and the mark of approval placed upon him before he may enter. * * * The acceptance of such suggestions is akin to a person bolting a particle of food, instead of masticating it. As a rule we bolt many a bit of mental provender, owing to its stamp of real or pretended authority. And many persons understanding this phase of suggestion take advantage of it, and 'use it in their business' accordingly. The confidence-man, as well as the shrewd politician and the seller of neatly printed gold-mines, imposes himself upon the public by means of an air of authority, or by what is known in the parlance of the busy streets as 'putting up a good front.' Some men are all 'front,' and have nothing behind their authoritative air—but that authoritative air provides them with a living."

The suggestion of associated manner, appearance and air—the "good front," in fact—is the principal element in the favorable First Impression. The balance is a mixture of tact, diplomacy, common sense, and intuition. But remember this always: the *best* "front" is the *real* one—the one which is the reflection of the right Mental Attitude and Character—the "front" of the Gentleman. If you lack this, the nearer you can act it out, the better for yourself. But no imitation is as good as the genuine article. The true Gentleman is the scientific mixture of strength and courtesy—the manifestation of "the iron hand in the velvet glove." So much for the First Impression.

The mental stages of Curiosity and Associated Interest on the part of the buyer are also to be induced by the Salesman in the Approach. We have described these phases in the chapter entitled "The Psychology of the Purchase," this particular part of which should be re-read at this point. A few additional words on these points, however, will not be out of place here.

Regarding the phase of Curiosity, we would say that it will be well if you can manage the opening talk to the prospect so as to "keep him guessing a little," while still holding his Associated Interest. Curiosity whets a man's interest just as Worcestershire sauce whets his appetite. The key to the arousing of Curiosity is the idea of "something new;" a new idea; a new pattern, a new device, etc. The mind of the average man likes "something new"—even the old fogy likes something new in his old favorites, new bottles for his good old wine. The idea of newness and novelty tends to arouse a man's inquisitiveness and imagination. And if you can start these faculties working you have done well, for Associated Interest is closely allied thereto. When you get a prospect to the stage of asking questions, either verbally or mentally, you have the game well started.

Never make the mistake of asking the man if he "wants to *buy* so-and-so." Of course he doesn't at that stage, particularly if you ask him in that way. It is too easy for him to say No! It is almost as bad as that stock illustration of adverse suggestion: "You don't want to buy any so-and-so, do you mister?" which brings a ready "No!" from the average person. Nor do you want to say: "I have called to see if I cannot sell you so-and-so, to-day, Mr. X." Or, "Can I sell you some so-and-so, this morning, Mr. Z?" This form of arousing interest is based on erroneous psychological principles. Of course, the prospect doesn't want to buy or be sold at this stage of the game—the sale is the finishing stage. This plan is like cutting a log of wood with the butt-end of the axe—you are presenting the wrong end of the proposition. You can never arouse Curiosity or Associated Interest in this way. Forget the words "You buy" and "I sell" for the moment—in fact the less you use them at any stage the better it will be, for they are too unpleasantly suggestive of the opening of pocket-books to be agreeable to the prospect. There are excellent substitutes for these terms—terms which suggest profit, advantage, saving and pleasure to the mind of the buyer, rather than ideas of expenditure and "giving up." Try to suggest the incoming stream of money to your buyer—not the outgoing one. The reason is obvious, if you understand the laws of suggestion and psychology.

In short, let your appeal at this stage be entirely to the Self Interest, Pleasure, and Curiosity of the prospect. Try to get him warmed up, and his imagination working. If you can do this he will forget his other objects of attention, and will lay aside his armor of suggestive defence and his shield of instinctive resistance to one whom he thinks "wants to *sell* something" and open his pocket-book. This is the stage in which you must get in the sharp end of your psychological wedge. Here is where you need the keen edge of your axe—the butt-end may be reserved for the Decision and Closing.

As far as possible, do not ask questions to which the prospect can answer "No!" at this stage. Fence him off on this point, and dodge every sign of a forthcoming negative. But if he does get out a "No!" or two—do not hear him. Let his "No!" slip off like water from a duck's back—refuse to admit it to your consciousness—deny it mentally—refuse the evidence of your ears. This is no time for "Noes"—go right ahead, unconscious of the words. Keep on appealing to his Interest, in the phases of Curiosity and Associated Interest. Your aim here is to get the prospect to the stage of Consideration. This stage is indicated by his asking a question showing a desire to know the particulars of your proposition. The question may show but a shade of interest, but it marks a move in the game. It is the prospect's answering move to your opening. It is an important psychological moment in the game. The next move is yours!

And that move is on the plane of the Demonstration—for the stage of the approach has now been passed.

Before passing on to the consideration of the stage of Demonstration, we desire to call your attention to the following excellent advice regarding the matter of rebuffs which are so often met with in the stage of Approach. It is from the pen of

W.C. Holman, and appeared in his magazine "Salesmanship." Mr. Holman says: "A crack-a-jack salesman will receive a rebuff as gracefully and easily and with as little damage to himself as a professional baseball player will take in a red-hot liner that a batter drives at him, and go right on playing the game as if nothing had happened. An amateur salesman will want to quit playing, or call the attention of the umpire to the malicious intent of the batter. A blow that would knock the ordinary man off his pins will do nothing more than to give a professional boxer a chance to show his agility and win applause. If you drop a plank on a cork in the water with a tremendous splash the cork will bob up as serenely as if nothing had happened, and lie quietly once more on the unruffled surface of the water. And so a clever salesman, when a smashing blow is aimed at him by a surly prospect, will merely sidestep gracefully and continue calmly with the prosecution of his purpose. * * * Self-control disarms all ill natured attacks."

CHAPTER 9

THE DEMONSTRATION

In the last chapter we left the Salesman at that stage of the Approach where the prospect manifests enough interest to ask a question or make an interrogative objection. This is an important psychological point or stage in the game, and here the Approach merges into the Demonstration on the part of the Salesman; and the stage of passive attention on the part of the prospect merges into that of active attention, discussion and Consideration. The moment that the prospect ceases to be a passive listener, and displays enough active interest to ask a question or make an interrogative objection, the great game of the sale is on in earnest. The Demonstration has begun.

This stage of the sale closely resembles a game of chess or checkers. The approach and preliminary talk of the Salesman is the first move in the game; the answer, question or objection of the prospect is the second move—then the real game or discussion is on. It is now "up to" the Salesman to make his second move, which is a reply move to that of the prospect. And this particular move is a highly important one in the great game of the sale. Like an important early move in checkers or chess the success or failure of the whole game may depend on it, so it is well to have this move mapped out as a part of your preliminary study.

Macbain truthfully says of the first remark of the prospect: "The customer is not going to commit himself in response to the first remark. He always holds considerable in reserve. An objection—either expressed or implied—can always be counted on. It may vary from a general 'busy' statement, or 'no interest in what is about to be submitted,' or it may be a specific statement—even heated, in fact—that the one approached has 'no time for the salesman or his house.'"

But, just as in chess or checkers there are certain "replies" indicated for every one of the first few opening moves, all of which are fully stated and explained in text books on these games, so in the great game of Salesmanship there are certain replies indicated for these preliminary moves on the part of the prospect. The large selling concerns have schools of instruction, personal or correspondence, in which the Salesman is furnished with the appropriate and logical answers to the objections and questions usually advanced by the prospect. It will be found that there are really but few moves of this kind in the game of the average prospects—they tend to say the same things under the same circumstances, and there is always an appropriate answer. The salesman will acquire many of these answers by experience, conversation with older salesmen, or by instruction from his sales-manager or the house. Each line has its own stock of objections, and its own stock of replies thereto.

There are two general classes of replies to objections, which apply to nearly every kind of proposition. The first is that of deftly catching the objection on your mental fencing-foil, allowing it to glance off, and at the same time getting a thrust on your opponent. President Patterson of the National Cash Register Company is credited with special cleverness in this kind of reply, and his salesmen are said to be instructed to listen carefully to the prospect's objection and then to turn it back on him by a remark based on the principle of: "Why, that's the very reason why you should," etc. In other words the objection should be twisted into an argument in favor of the proposition. In the hands of a master this form of reply is very effective, and often brings results by reason of its daring and unexpectedness. But it is not every one who has the skill to use it to advantage.

The second class of reply is based upon what is called indirect Resistance, which, by the way, is often the strongest form of *resistance*, and accomplishes its intended effect while avoiding the opposition and antagonism of Direct Resistance. Some writers on the subject have called this "Non-Resistance," obviously a misnomer for it is a form of resistance although subtly disguised. It is analogous to the tree that bends in order to avoid breaking under the blasts of the storm; of the flexible steel which bends to the pressure, instead of breaking as would iron; but both of which spring back into place immediately. It is generally very poor policy to directly oppose the prospect upon minor points—the main point is what you are after. And the main point is the order—the rest is immaterial and unimportant. Let us contrast Direct-Resistance and Indirect-Resistance, and see the points of each.

In Direct Resistance the minor objections of the prospect are met with the answer: "You are wrong there, Mr. X;" or, "You are entirely mistaken;" or, "You take the wrong view;" or, as we heard in one instance: "Your objection is ridiculous." The Direct Resistance is necessary in a few contingencies, or upon rare occasions, but it should be sparingly and cautiously used. It is a desperate remedy indicated only for desperate diseases. The Indirect Resistance expresses itself in answers of: "That is possibly *true* in some cases, *but*," etc.; or, "There is *much* truth in what you say, Mr. X, *but*," etc.; or, "As a general proposition that is probably correct, *but*," etc.; or, "I quite agree with you, Mr. X. that (etc.) but in this particular case I think an exception should be made," etc. The value of this form of resistance lies in the fact that it costs you nothing to allow the prospect to retain his own ideas and entertain his own prejudices, provided they do not interfere with the logic of your general argument, nor affect your main point, the order.

You are not a missionary or a pedagogue—you are just a Salesman and your business is to *take orders*. Let the old fellow keep his foolish ideas and intolerant prejudices, providing you can steer him straight to the ordering point. The active principle in Indirect Resistance is to get rid of his general objections in the easiest and shortest way, by allowing him to retain them, and concentrating your and his attention and interest upon the particular points of your proposition—the positive and material points of your particular case. Avoid disputes on non-essentials, generalities, and immaterial points. You are not striving for first prize in debate—*you're after orders*. Remember the legal principles of the "pertinent, relevant, and material" points, and side-track the "immaterial, irrelevant and impertinent" side-issues, even if you have to tacitly admit them in Indirect Resistance. Here it is in a nutshell: *Sidetrack and Sidestep the Non-Essentials.*

The Salesman has now reached the point in which the prospect is manifesting the psychological stage of Consideration—the stage in which he is willing to "look into" the matter, or rather into the subject or object of the proposition. This stage must not be confused with that of Deliberation, in which the prospect weighs the pros and cons of whether he should purchase. The two stages are quite different. The present stage—that of Consideration—is merely the phase of examination, investigation or inquiry into the matter, to see if there is really anything of real practical interest in it for himself. It is more than mere Associated Interest, for it has passed into the manifestation of interested investigation. In many cases the process never gets beyond this stage, particularly if the Salesman does not understand the psychology of the process. Many salesmen make the mistake of trying to make their closing talk at this point—but this is a mistake. The prospect must understand something about the details of the proposition, or the qualities and characteristics of the goods, before he uses his imagination or feels inclination to possess the thing. So here is where the work of explanation comes in.

The term "Demonstration" has two general means, each of which is exemplified by stages in the Salesman's work of Demonstration. The first meaning, and stage, is: "A showing or pointing out; an indication, manifestation or exhibition." The second meaning, and stage, is: "The act of proving clearly, by incontrovertible proof and indubitable evidence, beyond the possibility of doubt or contradiction." The first stage is that of "showing and pointing out"—the second, that of of "proof." The first is that of presenting the features of a thing—the second, that of logical argument and proof. And, therefore, remember that you are now at the stage of "showing and pointing out," and not that of "argument and proof."

Regarding the matter of "showing and pointing out" the features and characteristics of your goods or proposition, you should always remember that the prospect does not know the details of your proposition or article of sale as you do—or as you *should* know. The subject is not "stale" to him, as it may have become to you if you have not kept up your enthusiasm. Therefore, while avoiding needless waste of time, do not make the mistake of rushing this point of the demonstration and thus neglecting the important features. Better one feature well explained and emphasized, than a score hurried over in a sloppy manner. It is better to concentrate upon a few leading and striking points of demonstration, of material interest to the prospect, and to assume that he does not know anything about them except as he may show his knowledge by questions or objections—all this in a courteous manner, of course, avoiding the "know it all" air. The prospect must have time to allow the points to sink into his mind—some men are slower than others in this respect. Watch the prospect's face to see by his expression whether or not he really understands what you are saying. Better present one point in a dozen ways, to obtain understanding, than to present a dozen points in one way and fail to be understood.

In order to demonstrate your goods or proposition at this stage, you must have fully acquainted yourself with them, and also have arranged the telling points in a natural and logical order of presentation, working from the simple up to the complex. Be careful not to suggest *buying* at this point, lest your prospect take fright and lose interest in the demonstration. He is naturally in a defensive mood, for he scents the appeal to his pocket book in the distance—you must try to take his mind off this point by arousing his interested attention in the details of your goods or proposition. Explain the details just as you would if the prospect had called upon you for the purpose of investigation. In fact, if you can work yourself up to the proper Mental Attitude you may effect the psychological change by which the positions may be reversed, and so that it will instinctively seem to the prospect that he is calling on you and not you on him. There is an important psychological point here which you would do well to remember. The man who is called upon always has "the move" on the caller—if you can reverse this psychological condition, you have gained a great advantage. An awakened personal interest in the details of a proposition, on the part of the prospect, tends to reverse the conditions.

If you would understand what a scientific demonstration of an article or proposition is like, it would pay you to listen to the demonstration by a well- trained salesman of the National Cash Register Company. This company drills its salesmen thoroughly in this part of their work, until they have every detail fastened in their minds in its proper logical order. An old salesman of this company should be able to repeat his formula backwards as well as in the regular order—beginning at the middle and working either backward or forward, at will. He understands the "why" and "what for" of every detail of his article and proposition, and is taught to present them in their logical order. Listening to a talk of one of their best salesmen is a liberal education in demonstration.

The essence of this stage of the demonstration is that it should be given in the spirit of a conversational recital of an interesting story, or description of an event. Speak in an impersonal way; that is, avoid suggesting to the prospect that you are trying to sell him the thing. Let this part of your talk be given from the sheer enthusiasm inspired in your mind by the merits of your proposition. Let it be a labor of love—forget all about your hope of sale or profit. Your one aim and object of life, at that moment, should be that of inspiring the prospect with the wonderful merits of your proposition, which you yourself entertain. Yours should be the spirit of the propogandist seeking converts—imparting information for the good of others, and "for the cause." Forget the forthcoming collection plate, in the earnestness of your sermon.

The National Cash Register Company instructs its salesmen as follows regarding this stage of the demonstration: "When you have gotten a prospect to a demonstration you have accomplished a most important step. You can take it for granted that he is to some extent interested in the subject. Now, by all means make the most of that opportunity. Say what you have to say to him thoroughly and carefully. Don't rattle off your demonstration in a hurry, as if you were wound up and had to say so many words to the minute. Give him a chance to speak, to ask questions or make objections. He probably has certain ideas in his mind which may be a decided help or a decided hindrance to your argument. You ought to learn what they are. Don't imagine because he listens in silence that he agrees with you, or even understands all you say. Speak deliberately. If you see from a puzzled or doubtful look on his face that anything is not quite plain to him, stop and make it plain. Take time enough to explain each point thoroughly. Whenever you make a statement that is open to question, be sure to get his assent to it before you proceed. If he will not assent to it exactly as you make it, modify it until he does. Get him to assent in some degree to every proposition you make, so that when you get to the general result he cannot go back and disagree with you. Don't do this however as if you were trying to corner him, but with a simple desire to reach a reasonable basis of argument. Cast aside all attempts at being a clever talker, all idea that there is any trick of words or manner, any secret artfulness about selling registers, and put yourself in the plain, unaffected spirit of a man who has simply a truth to tell, and is bent upon telling it in the plainest, homliest way. Avoid above all things the fatal mistake of demonstrating to your prospect with a sense of fear, haste, and uncertainty. Realize fully the power of the facts behind you, and have the full confidence of your convictions; coolly and deliberately make each point clear and conclusive, and lead the prospect by simple steps up to absolute conviction."

If you have held your prospect's interested attention during this stage of the Demonstration, you will find that his imagination is beginning to work in the direction of making mental pictures of how the thing or proposition would work for him—how the article would look in his possession. It is a psychological law that interested investigation, or consideration, tends to awaken the interest of imagination and desire if the object of the investigation blends with the general trend of the person's thought and feelings. The very process of investigation inevitably brings to light new points of interest. And, then, the act of investigation and discovery, instinctively creates a feeling of proprietorship in the thing investigated or discovered. It establishes an association between the object and its investigator.

Halleck says: "* * * We must not forget that any one not shallow and fickle can soon discover something interesting in most objects * * * the attention which they are able to give generally ends in finding a pearl in the most uninteresting looking oyster. * * * The essence of genius is to present an old thing in new ways." And again: "When we think about a thing, or keep the mind full of a subject, the activity in certain brain tracts is probably much increased. As a result of this unconscious preparation, a full fledged image may suddenly arise in consciousness." Hoffding says: "The inter-weaving of the elements of the picture in the imagination takes place in great measure below the threshold of consciousness, so that the image suddenly emerges in consciousness complete in its broad outlines, the conscious result of an unconscious process." Halleck also says: "A representative image of the thing desired is the necessary antecedent to desire. Not until a representative idea comes to the mind does desire arise. It has often been said that where there is no knowledge there can be no desire. A child sees a new toy and wants it. A man notices some improvements about his neighbor's house and wishes them. One nation finds out that another has a war ship of a superior model, and straightway desires something as good or better. A scholar sees a new cyclopedia or work of reference, and desire for it arises. A person returns and tells his friends how delightful a foreign trip is. Their desires for travel increase. Knowledge gives birth to desire, and desire points out the point to will." In this paragraph we have quoted eminent authorities, showing the direct line of psychological progress from interested investigation, through imagination, to desire and will. One investigates and gains favorable knowledge regarding a subject; then his imagination operates to show him the possibility of its successful application to his personal case; then his desire for the thing is awakened.

The stage of Imagination is reached when the prospect begins to think of the thing or proposition in connection with himself. He then begins to picture it in its application to his needs or requirements, or in relation to his general desires, tastes and feelings. The Salesman, in order to awaken the Imagination of the prospect, should endeavor to paint "word pictures" of the thing in its workings, application, value, and utility. He should endeavor to make the prospect *see*, mentally, the desirability of the thing to any man—how it will work for good; how it will benefit one; how great an advantage it will be for one; how much good it will be in every way for its possessor. Avoid the personal application, even at this late stage—make the application general, so as to avoid scaring off the prospect's pocket book. The whole idea and aim of this stage of the process of sale is to awaken inclination in the prospect—to make his mouth water for the thing—to make him begin to feel that he would like to have it, himself. He must be put into the mental condition of the woman gazing longingly at the hat in the milliner's window; or of the boy who is peeking through the knot-hole in the fence of the base-ball park. He must be led into the feeling that he is on the outside of the fence or window—and the good thing is inside. He will then begin to feel the inclination or desire to "get on the inside."

We once heard a tale of two Southern darkies, which illustrates this point. The two were riding on the same mule's back coming home from work. The foremost darkey began relating the story of some roast possum he had feasted upon the preceding night. He pictured the possum as fat and tender; how they first "briled" him, and then roasted him in the oven; how juicy and brown he looked; how nice he smelt; how he was served up "wid coon-gravy poured all over him;" and finally how nice he tasted when the narrator dug his teeth into him. The darkey in the rear displayed increasing signs of uneasiness as the tale proceeded and as he imagined first the sight, then the smell, and then the *taste* of the possum. Finally he groaned, and shouted out: "Shet up, yer fool nigger! Does yer wanter make me fall clean offen dis yer mewel?" This is the point—you must make your prospect see, smell and taste the good possum you have, until he is ready to "fall offen de mewel."

Words describing action, taste, feelings, or in fact anything which relates to sense perceptions, tend to arouse the imagination. If the Salesman cultivates the art of actually seeing, tasting or feeling the thing in his own imagination, as he talks, he will tend to re-produce his mental pictures in the mind of his prospect. Imagination is contagious—along the lines of suggestion. Descriptions of sensations, or feelings, tend to awaken a sympathetic response and representation in the minds of others, along the lines of suggestion. Did you never have your imagination and desire fired by the description of a thing —didn't you want to see, feel, or taste it yourself? Did you never *feel* the effect of words like: "delicious; fragrant; luscious; sweet; mild; invigorating; bracing," etc., in an advertisement? How many young people have been hurried into matrimony by an illustration or word-picture of a "happy home;" "a little wife to meet you at the door;" "little children clustering around you," and all the rest of it? A well known instalment furniture dealer of Chicago is said to be psychologically responsible for thousands of weddings, by his suggestive pictures of the "happy home" and his kind statement that "We will Feather your Nest;" and "You find the Bride, and we will do the rest." The Salesman who can "paint bright pictures in the mind" of his prospect, will succeed in awakening the Imagination, and arousing the Inclination and Desire. Newman well said: "Deductions have no power of persuasion. The heart is commonly reached, not through the reason, but through the imagination. * * * Persons influence us, voices melt us, looks subdue us, deeds inflame us."

And so we pass to the stage of Inclination or Desire, by the road of the Imagination.

The mental state of Inclination, or Desire, following upon the arousing of the appropriate faculties through the Imagination which arises in the stage of Consideration, may be briefly described as the *feeling of*: "This seems to be a good thing—*I would like to have it.*" This Inclination has been aroused by demonstration and suggestion, and the prospect begins to experience the feeling that the possession of the thing will add to his pleasure, comfort, well- being, satisfaction or profit. You will remember the statement regarding Desire given in a previous chapter: "*Desire has for its object something which will bring pleasure or get rid of pain, immediate or remote, for the individual or for some one in whom he is interested. Aversion, or a striving to get away from something, is merely the negative aspect of desire.*" It is this feeling that you have aroused in some degree in the mind of the prospect. You have brought him to the first stages of Inclination, which naturally brings him to a deliberation as to whether he is justified in purchasing it, and to the point where he will begin to weigh the advantages and disadvantages of the purchase—the question of whether he is willing to "pay the price" for it, which is, after all, the vital question in nearly all forms of deliberation following Inclination and Desire. But as the prospect's mind passes to the stage of Deliberation, you must not lose sight of the question of Desire, for it may be necessary to re-kindle it in him, or to blow upon its sparks, when he debates the "to buy or not to buy." The Deliberation is largely a question of a conflict of motives, and Desire is a powerful motive—so you must be ready to arouse a new phase of "want to" in the prospect to counterbalance some other motive which may be turning the scales in the other direction.

In entering into the stage of Deliberation, or Argument, the discussion passes from the impersonal plane to the personal. The question no longer is: "Is not this a good thing?" to that of "Should you not have it for your own?" This is a distinct change of base, and a different set of faculties are now employed by the Salesman. He leaves the Descriptive phase and enters into that of Argument. He enters into that second meaning or phase of Demonstration which has been defined as: "Proving clearly." And the question of proof and argument is that of whether the prospect is not justified in acquiring the thing. The prospect's mind is already considering the two sides of the question, his Caution combating his Inclination. He is like "Jeppe" of whom we told you in a previous chapter. It is now a question of "my back or my stomach," with him. The Salesman's business now is to demonstrate to him that he can and should acquire the thing. This is a proceeding in which the Salesman's tact, resources, knowledge of human nature, persuasive power, and his logic are needed.

The Salesman has an advantage here which he often overlooks. We refer to the fact that the very objections of the prospect, and his questions give a key to his mental operations, which may be followed up by the Salesman. He knows now what is on the prospect's mind, and what are his general feelings, views, and inclinations regarding the matter. When he begins to talk he gives you a glimpse at his motives, prejudices, hopes and fears. It is quite an art to lead the prospect to ask the questions or to make the objections to which you have a strong answering argument. You then are able to turn back upon him his own argument. *It is a psychological fact that the force of a statement made in answer to an interrogative objection, is much stronger than would be the same statement made without the question or objection.*

Macbain says: "Lincoln, it is related, early learned in beginning the study of law, that he did not know what it was to prove a thing. By means of careful, conscientious study, in which he took up the problems of Euclid, one by one, he satisfied himself that he then realized absolutely what it meant to prove a proposition. One of the most eminent judges of the Iowa judiciary regards every legal problem as a proposition to be proved by a chain of reasoning. The salesman who determines with absolute accuracy what it means, first, to prove a proposition, and second to apply the general principles of demonstration to an immediate matter in hand, knows just how far to go in making his demonstration, what to include and what to exclude. He can see in his mind's eye the chain of evidence that he is fashioning and will make that fabric of his mind exact, logical and convincing."

(Note:—In order to train the student in logical thinking, development of the logical faculties, and the art of expressing one's thoughts in a logical and effective manner, we would suggest that he make inquiry regarding the volumes of the present series known as "The Art of Logical Thinking, or The Laws of Reasoning;" "Thought-Culture, or Practical Mental Training;" and "The Art of Expression." These books are published by the house issuing the present volume.)

It will be seen that the field of discussion in this stage of Deliberation covers not only the subject of the value and utility of the goods or proposition, but also the question of the price, the advisibility of the purchase at this time, the special advantages possessed, the over-balancing of assumed disadvantages, and in fact the whole question of purchase from beginning to end. The one thing to be held in the mind of the Salesman, however, is "*This will do you good; this will do you good; this will do you good!*" Keep hammering away at this one nail, in a hundred ways—hold it up to view from a hundred viewpoints and angles. It is the gist of the whole argument, at the last. Don't allow yourself to be sidetracked from this essential proposition, even if the argument spreads itself over a wide field. The point is that (1) *the thing is good*; (2) *the prospect needs it*; and (3) *that you do him a good turn by making him see that he needs it*. We once knew of a very successful life- insurance salesman who had but two points to his selling talk. These were: (1) "Life insurance is a necessity;" and (2) "My company is sound." He brushed aside all other points as immaterial, and insisted with all his heart and soul upon his two points. He was not an educated man, nor was he versed in the technicalities of life-insurance, but he knew his two points from cellar to garret. He outsold many men with actuarial minds, and extended knowledge. He followed the "rifle-ball" policy, instead of the "shot gun" plan. When he struck the target, he made a mark!

It is the Mental Attitude of the Salesman which is the power behind his argumentive rifle-balls. It is his enthusiasm which warms up the prospect's imagination and desire. And, back of these, must always be his belief in his own proposition. The Salesman must "sell himself" over and over again, as friend Holman has suggested. He must answer every objection which occurs to himself, as well as those which are thrust upon him in his work. If the goods are right, there must be an answer to every objection, just as there is a return-move to every move in chess—just as there always is "the other side" to everything. He must find this move, and this "other side" to every objection to which his proposition is open. And he must "sell himself" over and over again, as we have said. The National Cash Register people say to their salesmen: "Selling registers is a straight-forward serious work. You have a plain statement to make of the facts which you are convinced are true, and which you are certain it is for the prospect's benefit to know. You should be as sincere about it as if you were a clergyman preaching the gospel. If you go at it in this sincere spirit the prospect will feel the importance of what you say, and it will carry its due weight. It is a fact which you must fully believe, that the register is a great benefit to any man who buys it; that it will save any merchant many times its cost while he is paying for it."

Pierce says: "So in selling—it is absolutely essential to be genuine. First, last and foremost—be genuine. Practice absolutely what you preach. Be honest. Never undertake a line of goods that you cannot enthusiastically endorse. Otherwise you cannot 'sell yourself.' And selling one's self is by all means necessary. Students have asked us: 'How about being honest when the customer asks you a question that you know in your heart you cannot answer straight-forwardly?' The answer is: Drop that line; *the sooner the better*."

It is true that there are men who "wear the livery of heaven in which to serve the devil," and who practice self-hypnotization upon themselves until they get to actually believe that they are advocating an honest proposition in place of the "fake" they are proposing. And many of these "confidence-men" and "green-goods men" throw themselves so earnestly into their acting that they persuade their victims by reason of their earnestness. We remember Bulwer's tale of the French beggar whose tears wrought havoc upon the hearts of his susceptible victims. "How are you able to weep at will?" he was asked. "I think of my poor father who is dead," he answered. Bulwer adds: "The union of sentiment with the ability of swindling made that Frenchman a most fascinating creature!" But every genuine thing must have its counterfeit—the existence of the latter only serves to prove the former. The success of the "J. Rufus Wallingford's" of real life, are more than equaled by their final downfall. No man can continue to prostitute his talents and be happy, or even ultimately successful. The Law of Compensation is in full operation. No, we're not preaching—just indulging in a little philosophy, that's all!

Let us now proceed to the stage of the Salesman's Closing, and the prospect's Decision and Action.

CHAPTER 10

THE CLOSING

The "Closing" is a stage of the sale that is an object of dread to the majority of salesmen. In fact some salesmen content themselves with leading the prospect to the point bordering on Decision and Action, and then lose heart, leave the prospect, and later bring around the sales manager or special "closer" for the concern. They can lead the horse to the trough, but they cannot make him drink. While it is true that the stage of Closing is a delicate one, and involving as it does some practical psychological strategy, nevertheless we are of the opinion that many salesmen are victims of their own adverse auto-suggestions in this matter—they make a boogaboo of the thing which is often found to be but lath and plaster instead of solid iron and granite. Many a salesman is defeated in his Closing by his own fears rather than by the prospect. This stage of the sale is one in which the Salesman should draw on his reserve store of enthusiasm and energy—for he needs it in order to carry the day. As Holman once wrote: "General Grant said that in almost every battle, after hours of fighting, there came a critical moment in which both parties were tired out, and the side that braced up at that moment and pounded hard would win. This is probably so in selling. A good salesman knows that critical moment, and pounds."

The main cause of the failure to bring the prospect to a favorable Decision—the first of the two final stages of the Closing—is that the Salesman has not done his best work in the preliminary stages of the Demonstration. He has not demonstrated the proposition properly, or has not awakened the Imagination and Inclination of the prospect to a sufficient extent. Many salesmen slight the preliminary process of the Demonstration in their anxiety to reach the Closing—but this is a great mistake, for no structure is stronger than its foundation. The Closing should follow as a logical and legitimate conclusion of the preceding stages. It should be like the result of a mathematical problem which has been carefully worked out. Of course it is impossible for any one Salesman to "sell them all," from the very nature of things—but the average man could sell a larger percentage of prospects if he would strengthen himself along the preliminary stages leading up to the Closing, and to the final steps of the latter.

The gist of the whole matter of the failure of a prospect to make a favorable Decision is this: He hasn't been convinced! Why? If you can answer this question, you have the key to the problem. You haven't reached the man's desire. Why? If you can get him to "want" the thing, the decision is a mere matter of final settling down to choice. You may have said to the man, "This is a good thing—you ought to have it," over and over again—but have you actually made him see that it was a good thing and that he ought to have it? It is one thing to tell a man these things, and another to reproduce your own beliefs in his mind.

The changing of the talk from that affecting Deliberation on the part of the prospect, to that influencing his Decision, is a delicate matter. There is a "psychological moment" for the change which some men seem to perceive intuitively, while others have to learn it by hard experience. It is the critical balancing point between "enough" and "too much" talk.

On the one hand, the Salesman must beware of a premature Closing, and on the other he must avoid "unselling" a man after he has made the psychological sale. Some men are inclined toward one of these faults—and some to the other. The ideal Salesman has found the nice point of balance between the two.

If the Salesman attempts to make a premature Closing, he will probably have failed to bring about the full desire and careful Deliberation in the prospect's mind. As a practical writer on the subject has pointed out, this course is as faulty as that of a lawyer who would attempt to begin his closing address to the jury before he had gotten in his evidence. The trained finger on the pulse should detect the "high-tide of interest," and close the demonstration at this point, moving surely and swiftly to the Closing.

On the other hand, if the Salesman persists in talking on, rambling and wandering, after he has made a particular point, or all of his points, he runs the risk of losing his prospect's attention and interest, and with it the newly awakened inclination and desire. James H. Collins, in a recent article in "The Saturday Evening Post," relates the following amusing anecdote illustrating this tendency on the part of the Salesman:

"How easily a customer may be talked out of buying is shown by the experience of a real-estate promoter who sells New York property to investors in other cities through a staff of salesmen. One of his men reported that he was unable to close an elderly German in Pittsburg. 'I've explained the whole property,' said the salesman. 'He understands the possibilities, yet doesn't invest.' Next time the promoter was in Pittsburg he called on this investor, accompanied by his salesman. The latter explained the proposition again most exhaustively, and made every effort to be clear and convincing. * * * From time to time the investor tried to interrupt, but the salesman swept on, saying: 'Just a moment, and I'll take that point up with you.' When the story was finished he recapitulated. When that was finished he began a resume of the recapitulation preparatory to rushing the man. Here the boss felt that the investor really wanted to be heard, so he interrupted the salesman: 'Charlie, I guess if Mr. Conrad here doesn't realize the magnificent opportunities in New York realty after all you've told him, there's no use telling him any more.' 'Mein gracious!' protested Conrad. 'I do realize them. What I wanted to say is that I will take these lots.'"

There is a sixth sense, or intuitive faculty developed in many good salesmen which tends to inform them when they have said enough along any particular line, or on the whole subject. In the midst of a sentence, or after the close of a statement, one will notice a subtle and indefinable change in the manner or expression of the prospect which informs one that it is time to stop, and "sum up," or briefly recapitulate. And this "summing up" must be made briefly, and to the point, in an earnest manner. It should be made in a logical order and sequence, each point being driven in as with a sledge hammer of conviction. One should lay especial stress upon any points in which the prospect seemed interested during the Demonstration. In short he should fall in with the spirit of the attorney in his closing address, in which he sums up his strong points, always with an eye on the jury which he has carefully watched for signs of interest during the progress of the trial. Each juryman's character is represented by a faculty in the mind of the prospect—each should be appealed to along its own particular lines.

The perception of the "psychological moment" of closing the selling talk, is akin to that of the lawyer who leads his jury up to a dramatic and logical climax—and then stops. Avoid creating an anti-climax. Mr. Collins in the magazine article mentioned a moment ago says: "The chief shortcoming of the salesman who has difficulty in closing is, usually, that he doesn't know when the psychological moment has come to rush his man. This is a very definite moment in every deal. Veteran salesmen gauge it in various ways, some by the attention their argument is receiving, others by some sign in the customer's eyes, and others still by a sort of sixth sense which seldom leads them wrong. * * * If the mechanism of a representative sale could be laid bare for study it would probably approximate the mechanism of the universe in that material theory by which the philosophers explain the whole thing up to the point where a slight push was necessary to set it going eternally. The sale of the man who doesn't close is technically complete except for the push that lands the order. Sales may be made by patient exposition of facts, building up the case for the goods. But to close them, very often, a real push or kick is needed. Logic avails up to the moment when the customer must be rushed."

The trouble with some prospects is that they have practically made the Decision—but do not know they have. That is, they have accepted the premises of the argument; admitted the logic of the succeeding argument and demonstration; can see no escape from the conclusion—but still they have not released the spring of formal Decision which settles the matter with a mental "click." It is the Salesman's business to produce this mental "click." It is a process akin to "calling the hand" of the opponent in a certain game other than that of salesmanship. It is the stage in which the matter is fairly and squarely "put up" to the prospect. It is a situation demanding nerve on the part of the Salesman—that is apparent nerve, for it is after all somewhat of a bluff on his part, for although he wins if the prospect says "Yes," he does not necessarily lose if the answer be "No!" for the Salesman, like the lover, should never let one "No" discourage him. "Never take 'No!' for an answer," says the old song —and it is worth remembering by the Salesman.

The "click" of Decision is often produced by the Salesman "putting up" some strong question or statement to the prospect, which, in the popular term, "brings him to his feet." As for instance the closing illustration of some of the National Cash Register salesmen, who after having demonstrated the merits of the cash register by placing in it the "$7.16 of real money," in two-dollar bills, one-dollar bills, silver dollars, half-dollars, quarters, dimes, nickles and pennies, during the various points of the demonstration, turns suddenly to the prospect and says to him: "Mr. Blank, you have been watching every coin and bill I have put into this cash drawer. Now how much money do you think is in this drawer?" Mr. Blank naturally doesn't know. Then the Salesman proceeds: "Well, then, if you have no conception of the amount of money in this drawer, after watching me put every coin and bill into it, far more closely than you could possibly watch such transactions in your own store, you must admit you are guessing every night as to the amount that should be in your cash drawer in your store." Pausing a moment to let this strong point sink into the prospect's mind, the Salesman then says, earnestly and impressively: "*Mr. Blank, don't you think you ought to have a register of this kind?*" Every proposition contains features similar to the one noted above, which can be used effectively in bringing about the "click" of decision.

In some cases the Suggestion of Imitation may be employed at this stage by showing orders from others, provided they are of importance. Some men do not like this, but the majority are influenced by the example of others and the imitative suggestion prevails and brings down the scale of Decision. In some other cases the Salesman has found it advantageous to drop into a serious, earnest tone, manifesting a spirit akin to that of the earnest worker at a revival meeting, and laying his hand on the prospect's arm, impress upon him the urgent need of his doing this thing for his own good. With some prospects this plan of placing the hand upon him in a brotherly spirit, and looking him earnestly in the eye, results in the final warming up of conviction and decision—probably from the associated suggestion of previous solemn exhortations and friendly counsel. But other men resent any such familiarity—one must know human nature in using this method.

Never attempt to close your sale in the presence of outsiders. Always defer it until the prospect is alone, and you have his undivided attention. It is impossible to get into the "heart to heart" rapport in the presence of other people.

You may sometimes bring about the Decision by asking pointed and appropriate questions, the answer of which must act to clinch the matter. But in asking these questions always be careful not to ask a question which may easily be answered by a "No." Never say: "Won't you buy?" or "Can't I sell you?" These questions, and others like them give the suggestion of a negative answer—they make it too easy for the prospect to say "No." Remember what we have said elsewhere regarding the suggestions of questions. Remember the horrible example of "You don't want to buy anything to-day, do you?" And also remember that a question preceded by an affirmative statement, tends to draw forth an affirmative answer. As, for instance: "That is a nice day, isn't it;" or, "This is a beautiful shade of pink, isn't it?;" or, "This is quite an improvement, isn't it?" In asking the important question, do not show any doubt in your tone, manner or form of expression. Beware, always, of making a negative mental track for your prospect to travel over. The mind works along the lines of least resistance—be sure you make that "line" in the right direction.

In cases where you have been recommended to call upon a person by a friend with whom he has discussed the proposition, you may often find that but little preliminary talk is needed, and you may proceed to the Closing very shortly after opening the conversation. In these cases, the prospect often has "closed himself" without your aid—he wants the thing without urging.

When you meet this condition, take things for granted, and make the sale just as you would if the prospect had called upon you to make the purchase. And in any and every case, if you see that the prospect has "closed himself," clinch the matter at once. And you can readily see when this stage has arrived. After all, the process of discovering the "psychological moment" of Closing is like the intuitive discovery of the psychological moment for "popping the question" in courting. At certain times in courting these psychological moments arise—then is the time to "close." And the same rule holds good in Salesmanship. It is largely a matter of feeling, after all.

And, in Salesmanship, as in courting, remember also that "Faint Heart never won Fair Lady." Fortune favors the brave. When you feel the psychological urge of the moment—step in! Don't be afraid. Remember the old couplet:

> "Tender-handed grasp a nettle, and it stings you for
> your pains. Grasp it like a man of mettle, and it soft
> as down remains."

When it comes to the psychological moment, banish fear from your mind. Show spirit and be "game." You have got to make the plunge, and take the risk of "the proposal" some time—why not now? You have done your best, then go ahead. Stand up and take your chance like a man. But never act as if there is any chance about it—preserve your mental attitude of confident expectation, for these mental states are contagious.

If, in spite of everything, the Decision be against you, do not be discouraged. If you think you can reverse the decision by a little further persuasion, do so by all means. Many a battle is won, after it has apparently been lost. Few maidens expect their gallant laddies to accept the first "No" as conclusive—and the minds of many buyers work in the same way. There is a certain coyness about maids, *and prospects*, which seems to call for a little further coaxing. Many prospects yield only at the final appeal—they are like Byron's heroine who "saying she would ne'er consent, consented."

But if the "No" is final, take it good-naturedly, and without show of resentment, and assuming an "I will call again another day" spirit, bid the prospect good-bye, courteously, and take your departure. Many subsequent sales have been made in this way—and many have been lost by a show of ill- nature. The average man likes a game fighter, and respects a "good loser." Don't give up at anything short of a "knock-out," but, that given, shake hands with the victor good-naturedly, and then proceed to lay plans for another interview. Good nature and cheerfulness under defeat never fail to make friends, and to disarm enemies.

As we have said in a previous chapter, there is sometimes a hitch between Decision and Action. The spirit of procrastination creeps in, and the prospect tries to put off the actual order. Try to overcome this by "taking down" the order at once. Do not allow any wait at this stage. If no signed order is necessary get the order down in your order book as quickly as possible. Have your order book handy so that no awkward wait arises. Avoid these intervals of waiting as far as possible. Get through with the thing, and get out.

If a signed order is required, approach the request as a matter of course. Do not assume the air of asking any further favor, or of needing any argument regarding the signing. Treat it as a matter of course, and as if the matter had been agreed upon. Do not say "I will have to ask you to sign," etc., but say simply "sign here, please," placing your fountain pen at the "suggestive slant," and in his direction, indicating the line at the same time. Some salesmen even touch the pen to the line, starting the ink flowing and the suggestion operating with the one movement. Others proceed, calmly, like this: "Let's see, Mr. Blank, what is your shipping address (or street number)?" adding, "We can have these goods here by about such-and-such a date." And while he is saying this they are filling up the order blank. Then, in the most matter of fact, business-like manner they lay the order before the prospect, indicating the line for signature, and saying: "Now, if you will kindly sign here, please, Mr. Blank." And it is all over.

Always have the order blank, or book, and the fountain pen handy. Avoid fiddling around after the pen or the book, or both—

this is suggestive in the wrong direction. Some salesmen lay the pen on top of the order book, and place them easily before the prospect while talking. Others lay the pen by the side of the book, in the same way. Collins says: "One of the leading newspapers in the Middle West has a school for the canvassers who solicit subscriptions. A set of books is sold in connection with a year's subscription to this paper, and the solicitors are drilled in old fashioned bookselling tactics, learning their argument by rote. At the precise point where the signature of the prospect is to be secured the salesman is taught to take his pencil from his pocket, drop it on the floor apparently by accident, stoop over and pick it up as he finishes his argument, and put it into the prospect's fingers as a matter of course. Six times in ten the signature is written without more argument." The psychological point employed here is evidently that of distracting the prospect's mind from his ordinary objection, and attracting his attention to the recovered pencil. A similar proceeding is that followed by certain salesmen who carry a large fountain pen with a rubber band wrapped around the handle. Talking cheerfully, they drop the pen on the prospect's desk, close to his hand. The rubber band makes it fall noiselessly, and prevents it from rolling. The prospect is said usually to involuntarily pick up the pen, and move it toward the order book which has been deftly placed before him, and, then, still absorbed in the talk of the Salesman, he signs the order blank. These methods are given for what they are worth, and in the way of illustrating a psychological principle. Personally, we do not favor these methods, and prefer the orthodox fountain pen, courteously handed the prospect, at the "suggestive slant," with possibly the point touching the line as an illustration of the "on this line, please," which accompanies it.

The principle to be observed in all cases where orders have to be signed, receipts made out, etc., is to make the process as easy as possible for the prospect. Let him work along the line of the least resistance. Avoid giving him the adverse suggestion of "red tape," formality, "iron-clad contracts," etc. Act upon the principle of the young man who when he asked his father for money would say it very smoothly and *rapidly* "twenty dollars please," as if it were twenty cents. Smooth away every item of delay and friction, and adopt the "rubber tire and ball bearings" mental attitude and mode of procedure.

Regarding the much disputed and vexing question of the interval between Decision and Action, and the frequent failure of Decision to take form in Action—which question, by the way, is very important in the Closing of the Salesman—we ask you to read the following from the pen of Prof. William James, the eminent psychologist:

"We know what it is to get out of bed on a freezing morning in a room without a fire, and how the very vital principle within us protests against the ordeal. Probably most persons have lain on certain mornings for an hour at a time unable to brace themselves to the resolve. We think how late we shall be, how the duties of the day will suffer; we say, 'I *must* get up, this is ignominious,' etc.; but still the warm couch feels too delicious, the cold outside too cruel, and resolution faints away and postpones itself again and again just as it seemed on the verge of bursting the resistance and passing over into the decisive act. Now how do we *ever* get up under such circumstances? If I may generalize from my own experience, we more often than not get up without any struggle or decision at all. We suddenly find that we *have* to get up. A fortunate lapse of consciousness occurs; we forget both the warmth and the cold; we fall into some reverie connected with the day's life, in the course of which the idea flashes across us, 'Hello! I must lie here no longer'—an idea which at that lucky instant awakens no contradictory or paralyzing suggestions, and consequently produces immediately its appropriate motor effects. It was our acute consciousness of both the warmth and cold during the period of struggle, which paralyzed our activity then and kept our idea of rising in the condition of *wish* and not of *will*. The moment these inhibitory ideas ceased, the original idea exerted its effects. This case seems to me to contain in miniature form the data for an entire psychology of volition."

Prof. James, in another place, gives the following additional hint of the process of transmuting the Decision into Action: "Let us call the last idea which in the mind precedes the motor discharge, 'the motor-cue' * * * There can be no doubt whatever that the cue may be an image either of the resident or the remote kind."

It will be seen then that the "motor cue" which releases the spring of Action—the mental trigger which fires the gun of will—may easily be some remote idea *suggested* to the mind, as for instance the sight of the slanted fountain pen and order book. The man wants to, but does not feel like getting out of bed, and his mind becomes inactive on the question. If some friend had said to him, "Come, get out old fellow;" or if he had had his mind suddenly attracted by some outside sound or sight, he would have sprung out at once. As we have said, elsewhere, the placing of a piece of twisted paper in the ear of a horse will cause him to forget his balkiness—it changes his current of thought. Any new impulse will tend to get a man over his period of "I want to but I don't" mental hesitancy. We may have given you the psychology of the thing here—you must work it out in the details of application to suit your own requirements. Learn to show your prospect something that will cause him to spring out of bed. Learn to stick the piece of twisted paper in his ear, to overcome his balkiness. Give him the "motor cue" by supplying him with a mental image "either of the resident or remote kind." Like the boy shivering on the brink of the stream, he needs but a "little shove" to make him take the plunge. Then he will call to others: "Come on in, the water's fine."

And, now in conclusion: You have the signed order, but you must continue your Mental Attitude until you fade from the prospect's sight. Do not gush or become maudlin, as we have seen salesmen do. Maintain your balance, and thank your customer courteously, but not as the recipient of alms. Keep up his good impression of and respect for you to the last. Leave the prospect with this thought radiating from your mind: "I have done this man a good turn." The prospect will catch these subtle vibrations, in some way not worth discussing, and he too will feel that he has done well. Avoid the "Well, I landed this chap, all right, all right!" mental attitude, which shows so plainly in the manner of some salesmen after they have booked an order. The prospect will catch those vibrations also, and will not like it—he will resent it, naturally. In short, you would do well to follow the homely but scientific advice of the old salesman who said: "Keep your sugar-coating on to the last—leave 'em with a pleasant taste in their mouths." Make a good Last Impression as well as a good First Impression.

But—and remember this also—get away when your work is over. Do not hang around the office or store of the prospect after the sale is made. Do not place yourself in a position where some newly discovered objection will cause you to do your work all over again. You have got what you came for—now get out! As Macbain says: "When the close is made the customer should be left in the shortest possible time that may not be characterized as abrupt. Having 'talked a man into a sale,' the salesman should be careful not to talk him out. The old adage, 'Stop praising the goods after the sale is made,' is as true as it is trite." Collins very aptly says on this point: "The explainer type of salesman may actually sell goods to a customer and then, by staying and talking, unsell him without knowing it. * * * One afternoon not long ago, for instance, a salesman sold eleven thousand dollars' worth of fabrics to a prominent merchant and, by staying for a friendly chat after the order had been secured, gave the merchant time to think twice and cancel it. An excellent rule is that of a salesman who built up a business to a quarter million in competition with wealthy competitors, doing this by sheer selling ability. 'Take the first train out of town after you sell your man,' was his rule. If there was no train for several hours he excused himself the moment a deal was closed, and disappeared. 'Just as sure as I stayed around after that order was in my pocket,' he says, 'part of it would be cancelled or modified by the buyer, or some of my work in selling undone. If it were nothing else the buyer would play on the fact that I felt good about getting that order, and squeeze something extra out of me.' When you land your man get out of sight."

And, taking our own advice, kind reader, we, having said our say and "closed," will now take our departure. We thank you for your kind attention, and feel that we "have done you a good turn."